The CEO's Handbook – Upd Edition
How I Got There
by
J. Winsted White

Editing, Rose's Laws and Rose's Rules
of Business
by
Gary L. Rose

***
The Usual Disclaimers

The names of persons or corporations in this book are purely fictional in order to protect the innocent, and to keep me from getting sued. Although I have related most incidents and examples in the first person, many were told to me by others. I merely put them in first person, again, to put distance between me or them and any real persons or business entities. A few incidents were composites. Most, however, are true. I'm sure you'll form your own opinions of each.

Dedicated to the Past, Present and Future Memory of Bernard Madoff and all the Others Like Him

Many who become aware of this book will, no doubt, be of the mind that people like Bernie Madoff (Madoff Securities) Tony Hayward (British Petroleum) Roger Ailes (Fox News) Heather Bresch (Epipen) should go to heaven or possibly some other place and do so immediately if they haven't already. It is only in recent years that people like him have come into undeserved disfavor. Others quickly dismiss his contributions to our society.

Nevertheless, these companies made it possible for many of the "little people" to find new exciting careers in retail food, janitorial and tele-marketing services.

So it is with gratitude that this book is dedicated to their future memory. It is certain that history will undoubtedly treat them more kindly than today's fickle and ungrateful public.

Editor's Notes

I first met Jonah Winsted White in 2008 at a job group I had attended when I was trolling for potential clients for my executive coaching business.

At that time, Jonah was attempting to network with other job seekers by asking if anyone knew of a CEO's position that needed filling. Regrettably for him, he had little luck in this endeavor, but it afforded us the opportunity to meet and begin talking.

Quickly, I realized that he was the real deal, and thought we could team up to write a book that capitalized on his experience. This book, we surmised, could be the key to solving the unemployment problems in our country. What had worked for Jonah, could possibly work for others to stay employed, progress in their careers and for some, even climb the corporate ladder to the top.

Foregoing, are heretofore, the well-kept secrets of many a boardroom. I have also added many of the kernels of wisdom I have extrapolated from Jonah's experience as well as my own which I have titled "Rose's Rules of Business" and other principles I have illustrated in a series of tables. Enjoy and prosper.

Gary L. Rose
Editor

A Call to Worship

Somewhere in a house of corporate worship, a congregation sat in darkness in the first decade of the twenty-first century, now referred to as the Dark Ages of Human Commerce.

"All shall be mandated." and thus spake the great corporate god Ci-Eyoh.

"Ci-Eyoh is good, Ci-Eyoh is great, and so he has written." responded his subjects in unison.

"And all shall be for profits before mine eyes." commanded Ci-Eyoh.

"Ci-Eyoh is good, Ci-Eyoh is great, and so it shall be done." came the reply.

"And thus will all my people be so managed that the smallest of actions shall be proscribed." decreed Ci-Eyoh.

"Ci-Eyoh is good, Ci-Eyoh is great, so shall we do thy will." responded his subjects as one.

But one still, small voice disrupted the religious service. "But great and good Ci-Eyoh," the voice asked in the darkness, "what of initiative, creativity and spontaneity?"

"And so I have written," Ci-Eyoh admonished, "that initiative, creativity and spontaneity shall come forth as a wellspring on Tuesdays."

"So Ci-Eyoh has written, so shall it be measured." quaked his subjects in fearful response.

"But I do my best creative work on Wednesdays," the still, small voice persisted, "and only wish to serve you, good and great Ci-Eyoh."

"Initiative is mine!" thundered the great god Ci-Eyoh. And as the congregation became silent at the impudence shown towards their god, a great wind accompanied by a loud roar shook the assembly. A bolt of lightning struck the spot where the still, small voice had stood.

When it became quiet again, nothing remained at the spot except some ash in an empty cubicle.

"Ci-Eyoh is good, Ci-Eyoh is great. Let his will be done." Replied his subjects mechanically, lest they too, become ash.

The CEO's Handbook:
How I Got There
Narrative by
J. Winsted White
Editing and Commentary by Gary L. Rose

In the Beginning Was the Lie

I suspect, that if you go back far enough, you can remember some things from your youth that might have prepared you for the real world of business. The first example of this that I remember was when I was four years old.

My "sixty-something" widowed Grandfather lived with us, but I had noticed a pattern of his spending nights away from home. One day, as my father dropped him off at the Widow Gray's, he told me that Grandpa had to stay the night again to "help Mrs. Gray with the furnace." I gladly accepted this, but noticed when Grandpa was with the attractive forty-something Widow Gray, that they acted towards each other much as my parents did. I could tell that they were very good friends and that this was why he was willing to spend so much time helping her with her furnace.

Later, that year, when my father's failing business burned to the ground, I was told that an errant spark had caused the blaze. I do remember, however, overhearing my father asking his partner, Mr. Black, why the fire had started. Mr. Black had remarked "Noah, I didn't know how to start a flood."

So by the time I was eight, while not having any formal training, I'd at least had years of observing.   I should, therefore, typify myself with a decision I made while in the third grade. This was a critical moment in my life that formed the core of my character in finding gullible audiences and playing to them.

My third grade teacher liked to have me recite in front of the class. I hated it. I didn't want to be known as the teacher's pet. It was a sure-fire way to get beaten up at recess or on the way home.

One day, she asked me once again to stand in front of the class and recite from our reader. I did as I was told. Then she asked. "Now, Jonah, can you tell me what that means?"

I paused, looked at the faces of my classmates and read their expressions. I then turned to look at the teacher.

"I wasn't listening." I said. This was one of the first great lies of my career that I can remember.

The clear signal from the ensuing laughter was that I had gone from being a potential nerd and therefore, a possible object of derision, to being the class Smart Alec. The embarrassment I had caused my teacher, put me in good stead with my classmates. Naturally, I was sent to the principal's office, but I went gladly. It was preferable to getting beaten up by the other boys. This needs to be kept in the perspective of 1951, unlike today, when a child may not be scolded for any reason, lest the teacher be sued for harming the little shit's self-esteem.

The point of all of this, is that my early skills in "spinning" or handling a potentially harmful situation put me in a position of visibility. Consequently, people who didn't have these talents came to me and asked me to help them slither out of difficult situations they found themselves in. It didn't matter if I knew anything or not. They thought I did.

Only later did I realize that the ability to dissemble is the basic building block of management skills. The degree of sophistication we are capable of as individuals divides those of us who manage from those of us who are managed.

The ancient prophets understood this basic principle of adapting to our surroundings. The prophet Nachariah stated it best. "When in Crete, become a Cretin, but make sure you have skills." Or, stated simply, people have different talents and others will come to them when they have need of those talents. But lying is the most critical of all of those talents, whether by word or deed in order to blend in.

With this in mind, twelve apostles of the Fortune 100 companies met at the end of the 20th Century.

Their task was to develop principles of business for the 21st Century.

After meeting in the Summer of 1999 at St. Andrews in Scotland, they emerged a week later with what is now the bedrock of business knowledge now known as:

The Trump Syllogism

Major Premise
All successful business is built upon Bullshit.

Minor Premise
Learn to employ Bullshit and you will be successful

By observing the Trump Syllogism, not only will you survive, you'll begin learning the building blocks of how you become an effective CEO.

My Early Training: Dad's Paranoia

Before going any further, I have to explain my mindset and where I came from. My father, Noah Winsted White, was a principled guy. Many of the values I had to unlearn, I owed to him. He was the owner of a small manufacturing business before it was fashionable to be called a CEO.

One of his close friends used to say "Noah, you're a slow thinker, but you're a good thinker." He really wasn't a slow thinker, just careful. He liked to mull things over. And when he did, he was able to synthesize his own canons of life and business from a variety of sources. I realized later that they were just myths.

But he tried so hard not to get screwed, he ultimately and continually screwed himself. It took me years to understand these myths so that I could do the exact opposite.

Dad's Popular Myths

Myth Number One: Work Hard and you will succeed

Our culture is built on the practices of lying, cheating and stealing.

When I started my working career, I was under the assumption that a good education, hard work, and honor were valued and rewarded. In some cases, they were, but since the mid-eighties, this has proved the exception rather than the rule.

Despite the great experiment of a capitalistic society The liberal press is correct in stating that we are evolving into a two class system: The rulers and the ruled. The exploiters and the exploited. The real industrial giants of business are just the biggest and most successful examples of how things really work.

If you haven't already, this book will help you move into the class of people who do the exploiting.

The reality is that in order to be successful as a business leader, it is necessary that one learn the lessons I have documented in this tract early in their career.

The key to becoming a CEO is to get to the top, squeeze every drop of profit you can out of your business and not have to reinvest anything.

Development costs money. That erodes cash reserves, and in most cases is not necessary if all you're doing is running up the stock price based on projected revenues.

As a CEO, or a would be CEO, you need to make money in the short term, since there is no long term in American Business anymore. And in order to make money in the short term, you need to get it from someone else and let them worry about the next short term. It makes no difference if this adds to a company's long term debt. You, and perhaps even the next three series of CEO's won't be there when the debt comes due. But as CEO, in order to get the money from the next set of investors or your board of directors, you need to create the promise. This can be done in a variety of ways. I will cover them in the following chapters.

The underlying condition of business that makes all of this possible is that it is perfectly acceptable to not follow through on your projects. Just give the impression that you are.

If you want to get to be a world-class business leader, be it President, CEO, Chairman of the Board, or all three, you need to develop your skills at dissembling to the point where you actually begin to believe at least some of what you are saying.

As an example, almost every new software release or piece of new hardware is flawed in some way because it was rushed to the marketplace without being completely engineered or tested. We cut corners and hide defects. But rather than apologizing for this, we tell our stock holders that it is "good enough." We need to answer "current market needs."

We have rushed it to market because customers "demand it now." And we will "backfill with firmware, updates" or some other fancy name to euphemize defects.

At this point, your Marketing, PR and investor relations experts take these messages and rolls them out to the public.

This works because there is a little kernel of truth in each of these statements. As a CEO or future CEO, you need to realize that those persons and companies who can find those kernels of truth and build castles in the air around them are typically rewarded the best.

Now I don't claim to have any great credentials in terms of being a champion dissembler. And God knows I had to unlearn a lot of my early values. But if I can learn these critical skills, so can you. You don't have to be an MBA, just learn some of their tricks and employ them prudently.

Myth Number Two: Spell it All Out

I used to drive my father nuts. I wasn't, after all, considered as the brightest bulb on the tree, and with good reason. I had a tendency to simplify when he would go on for volumes and volumes during a presentation. He should have should have guessed when their eyes glazed over that it was overkill, but he just didn't get it.

I learned the hard way that simple, direct answers are best when addressing someone's business needs. If they want more information or specific examples, they'll ask, but they rarely do.

But there's a danger in this: If you tell them the truth in realistic terms, it will bite you on the ass. Instead, use as many qualifiers and euphemisms as possible, i.e. "our markets are now consolidating" instead of our sales are down.

This "less is more" concept of business communications has grown beyond its initial stages. In recent years, this has given rise to the usage of a number of quotable substitute phrases and management euphemisms in a new language that I have termed Synergistic Language to Improve Management Effectiveness.

Since this can be a mouthful, I'll refer to it from this point on, by it's acronym, SLIME. No one really knows where this language started but its use and its dialects have become the accepted standard in large corporations as a means of getting to the point while lessening the harsh-sound of business realities. Using SLIME, after all, is a somewhat more sophisticated form of dissembling.

As an example, rather than go on for volumes to my board of directors on a particular initiative, I've learned that there are all kinds of ways I can respond without having to tell the truth and keep my wording to a minimum. I'd like to share some of them with you:

Statement in SLIME	English Translation
It's in the concepting stage	Thought about it, haven't done squat.
Awaiting input from the field	I mentioned it to Jerry last week, I should probably ask him again.
In the initial draft stage	I scribbled some notes seconds before our meeting just so I could say this.
Was held in abeyance due to higher priority projects.	I took off last week to play golf.
Being held in abeyance due to higher priority projects.	I'm taking off *this* afternoon to play golf.

More on this later. I've devoted an entire chapter to SLIME.

Myth Number Three: "Somewhere in the middle is the truth."

The above statement, of course, is just politically correct Bullshit. When Dad couldn't reconcile two opposing points of view and didn't want to take sides, he started using the phrase "somewhere in the middle is the truth." In our business, it had to do with where you draw the line between standing your ground and yielding to pressure from customers who could make or break you. I interpreted this to mean that you need to remain flexible. Actually, he was kidding himself (yet another type of lying.)

The realities of our market were beginning to change, but he didn't understand what they were. When he started using this statement a lot in order to explain things to himself and others is when he decided to retire. Had he learned to stand astride both sides of an issue, he wouldn't have had to retire. Politicians have been doing this for centuries. It is only recently that American Business has adopted this technique.

As a recent example, about whether or not we should outsource, or internally staff up to meet new market demands our board was evenly split. As CEO, I didn't know which side would win, so I had my staff prepare a high-level PowerPoint for each case and then make vague statements to either side that were totally unintelligible, but could be interpreted to be either positive or negative. Then, when the board finally voted to outsource, I could truly say, "Well, as you know I've supported this position from the start."

Myth Number Four: "You don't get paid unless you produce"

Between my first and second years in college, I tried several different summer jobs. One of them was through an ad in the paper. It promised applicants as much as three hundred dollars a week to start. That was a lot of money then.

So I went to a meeting where a team of encyclopedia sales managers were recruiting young students like me to be salespeople. It seemed as if this was a total no-lose situation. All I had to do was work with the team canvassing neighborhoods. The plan was to work the small towns outside of the Twin Cities area, starting with St. Cloud, MN.

The company would train us and pay us $80 a week, and pay for our accommodations for the two weeks while we were training. Our training consisted of going door-to-door asking if we could present the product. After the presentations the families filled out an evaluation card which we would turn over to our team captain. A salesman would follow up a half-hour later to see if the family was interested in buying. We would get $20 for every set sold in addition to our $80 base.

The third week, we would become full-fledged salesmen ourselves, and would be paid $100 for every set we sold. We had to sell three sets per week in order to stay with the company. Doing some quick arithmetic, I figured that would be about $2,400 for the remainder of the summer, or about enough after taxes, to buy a new VW. (A brand-new Volkswagen in 1962 sold for just under $1900, including a radio.)

The only hitch was that we would have to wait until September to get paid. It took that long, we were told, to process and ship the orders, to receive the payment and so forth.

At the same time, my sales manager had just bought a brand new Chevy Impala Hardtop, complete with air conditioning. He boasted that he had paid cash.

He also confided in me that he got paid in cash weekly.

It dawned on me that I was wasting my time and needed to get a sales management job.

I promptly quit and tracked down the district manager for Encyclopedia Brittanica and applied for a job as a sales manager, having had experience working for one of their competitors.

He was glad to have me but told me that the only position he had available was in Des Moines, a four-hour drive from home.

At the end of the summer, I had made more than enough to buy a new Ford Galaxy myself and pay my University tuition and enough left over for books and all my other expenses for the year.

By the way, my friends who stayed with the first compnay got screwed. Over the Labor Day weekend of 1962, the office suddenly became vacated. My friends learned that the rent had been pre-paid from a check out of a mailbox in New Jersey, which had been closed in August.

Get a management job. That way, the people who work for you have to produce. All you have to do is keep up the pressure on them. You get paid no matter what.

Myth Number Five: "Play dumb and play along."

Dad always used to tell me "You're the perfect company man. You're as dumb as they are." Don't take this literally. He didn't mean it that way. It had to do with my inexperience. He said it good-naturedly to make his point, and his brother, my revered late Uncle Stark who was ten years older than Dad, had said it to him. So he used it to find common ground between us. Clearly, he had contempt for big companies, government and politicians and anyone who worked for them, not that he ever had.

But he'd spent time in the Army Air Corps, and figured it was about the same thing. The one piece of truth that he'd observed, was how everybody seemed to go along with a bad idea like a bunch of sheep. People took on good faith, ideas and programs that their guts told them were stupid. How many business activities have you seen in your lifetime that were fools' errands? To make matters worse, people who know better, lie to their bosses when they go along with them rather than risk their jobs. In this respect, he was right about big companies and government being the same. There he made the leap from the specific to the generic. If your instincts tell you to go along, just do it.

Here is what I learned: Play dumb long enough and you won't be playing anymore.

If you want to be in control, surround yourself with enough people who do play dumb. They will continue to play dumb and support your position just to save their own meaningless jobs.

Myth Number Six: Cover every detail

When I hired on at my first Fortune 500 company, I was a little intimidated. I believed everything I'd ever read by the Peter Druckers, of the world. This included a lot of myths about the intelligence level of people in top positions in big corporations. So I was prepared to work very hard in order to play with this bunch of whiz kids.

My first project was to do a national promotion in twenty-five test markets. I researched like crazy. I had the demographics. I had the spending habits. I had the brand preferences. I had all of it. I lost my audience in the first five minutes of my analysis. The VP of marketing began drumming his fingers. "Which fifteen markets would you pick, and how much will it cost?" he asked. I flipped to my last two slides and gave him the answer.

All they really wanted were the advertising pages, or "tear sheets" from the newspapers for their salesmen. The salesmen could then show customers that we had done this program in fifteen of the largest US markets.

There was no way I could have known this, but I watched others and learned.

It's sort of like one of those Marine Corps Jody calls when you're marching. Just grunt "Minimum investment, Sales Growth, ROI, and Next Quarter." In between, show lots of graphics, preferably in PowerPoint on a very large UHD Curved Flat Screen.

Here's what I learned: Tell them what they want to hear.

Truth to any governing body in a business is what they want to hear, or are willing to believe. So in order to make your points, you must first find out what it is that they want, and then invent your story to fit their pre-conceived notions.

How business operates

The forgotten simple basics

So how does business really operate? Unfortunately, there are so many books out there by "experts" going about the task of legitimizing how business operates, it only confuses us. I'm talking about those who write new chapters on things like reengineering, throughput, and so forth. It's all more Bullshit.

The Eastern South Dakota Business Journal recently quoted the following: "The National Congress of Business Experts state that if current trends hold true, by the year 2020, one out of every three people in the United States alone, will be business process experts. The market will grow to accommodate them."

The Four Function Test - Here's how a successful business is supposed to operate:

1. It finds a need in the market for a product or service.

2. It makes the product or service

3. It sells the product or service

4. It makes a profit on that product or service

Making money is "IT," capital I, capital T. All else is embellishment, because every action within a company should support at least one of these four functions. I have a simple test that I give to new prospective employees. I ask them to take a stab at what they think the mission of our company is. I've seen all kinds of answers, ranging from "providing a better quality of life to users of...," "Creating new, innovative..."

The list goes on. Every once in awhile, someone answers, "To make money. Everything else is just how we do it."

When I hear this, I know that the applicant can read the Bullshit and has cut to our core value. So I hire the applicant. What I've also heard is the applicant using the term "we," indicating that he is already thinking in terms of where he needs to place his loyalty.

Perception is the new Reality
This concept in the 21st Century has now changed the four function test.

The 21st Century Updated Four Function Test - Here's how a successful business actually needs to operate:
1. It creates and promotes a perceived need in the market for a product or service.

2. It makes a product or service that is perceived to fill that need.

3. It sells the product or service at an outrageous price, the higher the better i.e., overpriced vacuum cleaners, audio speakers and body lotions.

4. It makes what shareholders or potential investors perceive as a huge profit on that product or service.

The next four chapters will discuss some basic truths of how businesses deal with this prime directive by lying creatively to their customers, their employees, their stockholders and themselves.

Is IBM really in business to create harmony in the Universe?

Will Bob's Computer Parts feel it has been a failure if it hasn't created a warm and loving place for its employees to work?

Of course not. Then why do these businesses spend so much time espousing such false values? I have called upon my experience as a CEO, and the experience of those I have worked for before becoming a CEO, whose techniques I admire, respect and have learned great lessons from to explain these apparent inconsistencies.

How to Maximize Your Bonus as CEO When Revenues Decline

CASE STUDY 1: Meg-Orifice Corporation

Taking care of yourself before all else is really the first priority of a CEO. That's why this chapter is near the beginning of this book. All else supports that goal.

At some point after you become CEO, your company's revenues will decline. This may be temporary or it may point to an increasingly downward trend. Most likely, it will be a reflection of your poor business skills or poor grasp of what it is you are supposed to do. Not to worry. This is normal.

After my installation as CEO, Meg-Orifice, a medical device company, was quite profitable for a number of months. So much so, that there was this barrel of cash I kept in a corner of my office. But the little people, as they typically do, wondered why their pay had been frozen and there were never any bonuses or profit sharing if our products were doing so well and sales continued to increase. Clearly, we needed to get them to stop complaining, so one day, I decided it was time to do some fun things with a little bit of the extra money to get them back on board.

The first employee placation program was "Cake Day." This tactic was first documented in 1988 by J. Trimmel of Transcontinent Manure Brokerage of Birmingham, Alabama, as an incentive to make his little people feel important too.

Normally cake day had been only for the big "muckety-mucks", but expanding it to all employees was seen as truly enlightened. Once a month, in the company lunchroom, one chocolate and one vanilla sheet cake would be provided for such events. It was a "help yourself" deal, during which time, anyone could go into the lunch room, and after depositing a dollar in a coffee can, could help themselves to a piece of celebratory cake while singing "Happy Birthday to Me."

I can't begin to tell you how special that made the little people feel when their birthdays or anniversaries, or whatever other of their meaningless occasions rolled around. It was also self-funding, so that I could replace the money that had been spent on the cakes in my barrel.

I next told my VP's to form a team to develop a set of "higher" goals for the company to achieve as well as the normally stated ones. In a spurt of genius, after having roughed out something about how the new Corporate America was becoming a more "touchy-feely' place, I directed the team to come up with a set of principles that they could have made up into plaques, brochures and clever, colorful screens that would pop up at random on employees' computer monitors, and so forth. Here's how the team stated the goals:

- Our company will make a statement to our customer physicians and their patients by developing the highest quality products and services we can attain.
- We will provide a wholesome, cheerful workplace for our

employees and provide the appropriate environment for their personal growth.

- We will contribute to the general well-being of the community, by encouraging support of those institutions that enhance the quality of life.
- We will continue to return a reasonable profit to our shareholders, and ensure their investment in our future.

The team employed our senior-most Bullshit writer to develop the platform for this. But I ran into a problem here. It backfired because some of my senior management team began taking some of them seriously. Consequently, they had forgotten their original purpose, to feign these values, rather than actually adopt them. Subsequently, it took on a life of its own and generated the following action items that regrettably began digging into my cash barrel:

An art committee was formed to spend some of the money and decorate the halls. Thus, three-hundred thousand dollars was spent on art.

A committee was formed to develop a more ecologically correct environment within the building. One-hundred and twenty-five thousand dollars was taken out of the cash barrel and spent on oxygen-producing house plants.

A star panel was formed to choose programs on public television that the company would sponsor. An annual budget of two hundred and fifty-thousand dollars was approved to sponsor programs on the local educational channel. This included what we used to call Institutional Advertising, where we didn't hawk the product, but rather our company statement of being "quality."

My management team "volunteered" me to chair a subcommittee for United Guilt, "Home Equity Loans for the Homeless." (Based on home equity, of course.) Then I thought that this might be something nice I could add to my own resume as a "do gooder," so I also started an annual company program, and mandated goals of 2% of annual gross salary per person; one-percent from each employee, and a matching one-percent from the company (but not out of my cash barrel.) You may remember United Guilt best from some headlines two decades or so ago, when it's CEO, Worthington Acrimony, formerly a fellow member of CWBCEOCA (Completely White Bread CEO's Club of America,) went to jail for embezzling funds.

I thought maybe they were going to insist that we also put money into research and development of new products, perhaps look at new markets, or maybe even into incentives for some "intrapreneurship" enterprises. Fortunately none of this happened. If it had, it would have taken money that I had mentally reserved in my mind for CEO performance bonuses.

One year later, while not exactly going in the tank, company profits had dropped by one-million, five. My board of directors had a hissing-fit, but I told them that I had a quick fix for this.

The houseplants were now a liability of $25,000 per year, for maintenance. So I gave them away to charities (for a full write-off), and had them replaced with fake plants, from Wal-Mart financed by selling off the art, which had doubled in value in just fifteen months.

I pulled sponsorship for all but one of the public TV programs.

I was now established as a big shot in United Guilt, so I mandated that the employee base contribution continue with the program, but pulled the corporation's matching funds so that our employees had to double their contribution. This saved us some big bucks that dropped to the bottom line.

But that still wasn't enough. So I asked HR what they could do. They came up with twenty low-level positions that no one would notice had been cut, with an average cap of nearly $38,000 including salary and benefits that could be eliminated. This picked up another $750,000.

If you do some quick math, this added up to $1,465,000. With a little tweaking here and there, the shortfall had more than been made up, and I was able to increase my annual bonus.

Our overall revenues were just a tad short of the previous year's, but I'd made a case for "shifted" business coming in after the first of the year. Consequently, they couldn't nail me with an apples-to-apples comparison. A perceived "reasonable profit to our shareholders" had been achieved.

As a result, I had no trouble convincing the board to vote me the reserve of $500,000 in cash and another $800,000 in 90-day liquid incentive stock options as my performance bonus.

Now, whether you are already a CEO, or even if you are only a Division President or VP think about where you work.

- What is your chief goal?
- Where do you fit into that goal?
- Would 20, 30, even 100 mid-level employees be missed?
- How long would it take to replace them with lower-paid employees?
- Could you outsource them?
- Could you off-shore them?
- Would these steps be enough to attain your bonus?

Exercise

Now, the point here, isn't to determine actual growth, or actual profit, but to find that point at which you, as an executive are compensated and adjust your P&L to reflect that perception.

So, considering this, if revenues or profits or both go down:

How many people do you have to fire to make up the deficit in profit? Remember, the key here, is for there to be a profit so that you can get your compensation and bonus.

How can you make this process repeatable in subsequent years?

Rose's Rule of Business #1: Have an Exit Strategy

Milking a "cash cow," is really the objective. Developing tomorrow's markets is Bullshit. As a top executive and shareholder, you shouldn't plan on being around that long. Therefore, no matter what your company says is its chief goal, remember this; Your board expects you to make money for them now. You need to determine how long "now" can last and not be present when it ends.

V. How to Exploit Your Employees' Productivity

CASE STUDY 2: Business Synergistics, Inc.

I have to step back quite a number of years in my career, before I was a CEO to pay tribute to someone I worked for. As a mature, but still young executive, I worked for a promotion house, Business Synergistics, Inc., "B.S. Inc." for short. We produced Bullshit. Others called it productivity programs, incentives, and marketing communications. It was all crap, of course, but American Business loves crap.

At this point in my career, I had gone from doing engineering work, to the selling and marketing of engineered systems. This meant spending time educating people on the features and benefits of the systems I had engineered.

Therefore, I hired on as the director of the Business Communications Group. The company had a reputation for burning through middle-management and executives in a one or two year cycle. I knew that, but wanted to work there anyway, since they had a reputation for their productivity programs being "breakthrough" Bullshit. This was during that golden period of "corporate culture." So it was good to have a short stint at B.S. Inc. on one's resume. And truly, one was never assured of anything more than a short stint because of the burnout environment.

The philosophy of these productivity programs started right within B.S. Inc. They took great pains to give the impression of how important the employee was to the organization. They even produced their own Bullshit to promote this idea. This was, perhaps the best example of internal marketing prevarication I have ever seen within a company. The programs that worked were then cloned and rolled out to customers.

Suborning Employees For the greater good

As part of my indoctrination, I spent a morning with the President and Owner, Axel Hoel, affectionately referred to by his employees in hushed tones as "Ax Hoel," or just "The Big A.H." I then had to spend a half-day with each of the Vice Presidents, with whom I would work. They were to tell me in "their own words" what each department was all about.

So I spent a half day with Bill Schulz, V.P. of Sales.

"I'll tell you, Jonah," he said " this is the best place I've ever been. I guess in my own words, it's about Sacrifice, Service, and Commitment. You could say that we're all happy to work under the policy of HESS…we work holidays, evenings, Saturdays and Sundays, or whatever it takes to get the job done for our family, and B.S. Inc. is a family."

After that I spent a half day with Bob Sherwood, V.P. of Finance.

"I'll tell you, Jonah," Bob mused " this is the best place I've ever been. I guess in my own words, it's about Sacrifice, Service, and Commitment. You could say that we're all happy to work under the policy of HESS…we work holidays, evenings, Saturdays and Sundays, or whatever it takes to get the job done for our family, and B.S. Inc. is a family."

Next, I saw Bud Schoberg, Corporate Counsel.

"I'll tell you, Jonah," Bud offered " this is the best place I've ever been. I guess in my own words, it's about Sacrifice, Service, and Commitment. You could say that we're all happy to work under the policy of HESS…we work holidays, evenings, Saturdays and Sundays, or whatever it takes to get the job done for our family, and B.S. Inc. is a family."

And finally, I spent time with Bert Schumacher, V.P. of Corporate Communications.

"I'll tell you, Jonah," Bert opined " this is the best place I've ever been. I guess in my own words, it's about Sacrifice, Service, and Commitment. You could say that we're all happy to work under the policy of HESS…we work holidays, evenings, Saturdays and Sundays, or whatever it takes to get the job done for our family, and B.S. Inc. is a family."

At this point, I and one other new executive hire were "invited" to dinner with our wives, by The Big A.H. and his wife, B.G. This was a mandatory performance that started at The Big A.H.'s house. "B.G." is what she called herself, although The Big A.H. called her "Barbie." Turns out her name was Barbra Gayle. She'd gone by both. At B.O. we all affectionately referred to her as "Babs" although she hated it.

I'm not sure what I had expected, but when I arrived with my wife, Madeline, we were surprised. Oh, it was a big enough house, but it was in disrepair. There was a dump truck sitting in the driveway, and none of the foliage had been trimmed in about ten years.

We walked up to the tattered screen door and rang the doorbell. It didn't work. I knocked, and Axel came bounding to the door.

Once inside for cocktails, there was old orange shag carpet on the floor, the curtains were old orange shag velvet. There were velvet paintings on the walls and muskets crossed over the fireplace. The sofa was made of a type of orange shag, and finally there was The Big A.H.'s dog, a mangy, smelly orange hound. It all belied his status as the CEO of a multi-million dollar corporation. In fact, I felt sorry for him, thinking he must be giving all the profits to his employees.

After cocktails, a ride in his old Cadillac with orange shag seat covers and non-working air conditioning, to a run-down roadhouse out in the country, continued the impression I was getting.

Madeline just sat through the whole thing, took it all in and as always, was the perfect partner. I couldn't read her. But that was good. It meant they couldn't read her either.

During dinner, Babs kept asking Madeline about things like church, how she felt about divorce, (she and The Big A.H. were each other's third marriage,) how she felt about my working long hours and traveling a lot. In the meantime, Axel worked on me, while smiling and patting me on the behind. Earlier, I'd gotten a warm feeling about the new boss, but was now, somehow, getting mixed messages.

When dinner was over, we returned to the unkempt house, demurred on after dinner drinks and after a short game of Twister on Axel's orange shag carpet, we went home. I still didn't get it; the house, the grounds, the dump truck. I wondered if the business, for all of its activity, was really on the skids and if I had made a bad career choice.

"It's all an act" Madeline said during the forty-minute ride home. She had it figured. "It's a set up to work your rear-end off. Did you see that rock on Barbara's finger? And that dress was a Versace. I'll bet he's got a real mansion somewhere. Barbara wouldn't live in a dump like that. Nor would I, for that matter."

How to Use a Monthly Crisis to Scare the Shit out of Your Employees

So when I got my first real clue a week or so later, I was semi-prepared for what happened. Apparently every month Axel held an all company meeting in the warehouse to extol the virtues of the organization, and tell employees how they were doing. I had been informed, however by some of the more experienced of the crew, that no matter how well we were doing, we were always told of some new crisis in some market that might affect our business.

This meeting proved to be no exception. There was a crisis. But we were told in such a nice way, that no one could really complain. The Big A.H. had his VP's stationed at the five warehouse doors passing out Hershey bars to everybody. We were informed that we would have to work harder, and make sacrifices, come in on Saturdays, evenings, etc. so that we could produce more Bullshit for our customers or possibly lose some of them, hence some jobs could be at risk. I got a Hershey with almonds. At the time, it was my favorite.

During our November meeting, we were told that with any luck, by Christmas, we would have met our corporate objectives. Things were looking good, not to worry, but not meeting the challenge could put some jobs at risk. We just had to pitch in a little harder. I was presented with a Nestle's Krunch.

Immediately prior to Thanksgiving, our second emergency meeting for November was called. We were told that we would have to redouble our efforts, and that for those of us who were really committed, perhaps the Friday and Saturday after Thanksgiving would see us at our desks. Of course, if we didn't put out the extra effort, jobs could be at risk. We were each given a frozen turkey as a sign of good faith. This was not all bad. Even though business was tough, Axel had a benevolent side to him.

Apparently, a lot of other people thought the same thing. We all worked that weekend and produced an enormous amount of junk mail for our customers. We developed product that had been scheduled to take up the entire first quarter of the following year. We had done well for The Big A.H. and he appeared happy.

At our warehouse meeting the week before Christmas, we were told that although we had met our "stretch" objectives, new tax laws passed earlier in the year had produced unforeseen results. This unfortunate occurrence meant that there would be a shortfall to contribution (profit). Eighty-seven employees were laid-off two weeks short of year-end bonuses. This included eight, ten-year and 23 five-year veterans. The rest of us were given boxes of Danish butter cookies.

On January 4, ads went into the local paper to fill newly created positions with new job descriptions. At first I didn't get it and then it sunk in. On the surface, the titles appeared different, but underneath, they were the same old jobs, just at lower starting salaries than those who had been terminated. We'd gotten rid of a lot of talent, and would have to train all new people.

I stayed with the company for two years. During that time, I received seventeen candy bars, two turkeys, two boxes of Danish cookies, a box of chocolates, and finally, my notice. In two years, the pattern never varied. More about that later. They would hire a new batch, burn them out, pitch them in the creek, and go on to the next. The system in and of itself, was pure genius.

It took a full two years before I finally learned the truth about The Big A. H. from one of his newly-fired vice presidents. Madeline had intuitively known it all along. The house, dog, dump truck, all belonged to Axel's groundskeeper. The mansion, which shared the same address as the groundskeeper's house was a mile further down the road. None but a handful in his personal cadre had ever seen it.

Whenever the cuts came, most of this cadre seemed immune. The goal here, I decided, was that if I were ever in a similar position again, I should make it a point to try to get invited to the main house.

Exercise:

- What untruths could your top management develop to further the goals of the company?
- Will these untruths trigger the "pucker" reflex in your employees
- Are these untruths strong enough to continually scare the shit out of them and keep them desperate to produce at a maniacal level
- How could they influence employee productivity in other ways?
- Can you let some of them go once in awhile just to reinforce the message?
- Can supervisors' work be duplicated at a lower level to cut more bodies?
- How much could this save the company?
- Does this then lower the cost of production in hourly terms? By the project?
- How much harder will employees work for cheap incentives versus actual dollars?
- Can you regularly distribute candy bars instead of pay raises?
- Can you use T-shirts, or perhaps even jackets to replace bonuses?
- Finally, figure out how cheaply you can buy jackets or T-shirts?

Rose's Rule of Business #2: Keep your employees scared shitless.

Any internal motivational program you implement in relation to your employees, no matter how benevolent you would like it to appear, should have only one purpose; To give the employee a false sense of security in order for you to exploit him or her.

VI. Espousing Trust Without Having To Do Anything Trustworthy
CASE STUDY 3: Mega-Flush Corporation

I learned a lot about trust at Mega-Flush that helped me become a CEO later in my career.   The word "Trust" is real big in business-to-business partnerships. I'm not saying that there is any, just that companies keep using the word to sucker each other. The reason for this is that once one of the parties is convinced to be trusting, the other can then move in for the kill. This is life at its most basic.

Keep in mind, however that while your employees are doing it to your customers, you should be doing it to them.

When I worked for Mega-Flush, a company that manufactured plumbing products, we had a direct sales division, and also sold through distributors all over the country. Most of these distributors carried long lines of products that were sold to a variety of customers including the construction business, independent contractors and, of course plumbing companies. Ours was only a small percentage of their business, but presented the potential for at least ten times our annual volume.

The key was to get the distributors to concentrate on those customers who bought our products.

- We had established distributor levels and incentives for them at these various levels:

- $ 50,000   in annual purchases = Copper Plunger Award Plus 500# of Caustic Acid
- $100,000   in annual purchases = Bronze Plunger Award Plus 1000# of Caustic Acid
- $250,000   in annual purchases = Silver Plunger Award Plus 2000# of Caustic Acid
- $500,000   in annual purchases = Gold Plunger Award Plus 5000# of Caustic Acid
- $1,000,000 in annual purchases = Platinum Plunger Award Plus 10,000# of Caustic Acid
- Top Distributor in U.S. = Diamond Commode Award Plus 40,000# Truckload of Caustic Acid
-

Part of our company culture at that time was to exclaim at every trade show or marketing event how very grateful we were for having customers, keeping in mind that in business, gratitude is the shortest-lived sentiment. This was true whether it was the annual meeting of the Bidet Retailers of Alabama, or that giant of all associations, the Consortium Of Wholesale Toilet Underwriters, Retailers and Distributors, (COWTURD)

We were told to act dumb and ingenuous, although for many of our salesmen this was no problem. And if we did it long enough and hard enough, some of these distributors would actually believe we had no clue that business was a predatory sport.

Everything in our company doctrine, told how we lived and breathed for our customers. Like many companies in the eighties, we called this philosophy "Focus on Understanding Customer Knowledge Enabling Merchantability" (FUCKEM.)

Let me explain, but first point out that at that early point in my career, I had taken such directions at face value without much thought to any sinister underpinnings. That's because it's just "business," and not "personal." And business is all about perpetuating itself, just like any life form. I guess that I've known that all along.

Ever the company man, I threw my heart into it. I traveled all over the country and learned our distributors' businesses with an eye to subverting their customer bases.

I looked for the soft spots in their markets with relationship to our products and then developed a number of tools they could use to reach the customers who might be interested in our specialty products. For example, in certain parts of Louisiana, in the home builders market due to spicy foods and rampant obesity, there was a latent demand for our industrial strength Magnum series with captive air-assist flush. This premium commode, normally installed only in the best of hotels, was hardly known to the consuming public prior to our coop advertising program.

But I digress.

Our program even included categories of products other than our own. Innocently, we told them that it was all done in the spirit of enlightened self-interest.

The programs I developed included customizable materials like product videotapes, print ads, broadcast commercials, printed brochures, catalogues and marketing plans that we developed at our expense. We furnished these at no cost so that each distributor could tailor them to his own business. We also established a training program to teach distributors to use these marketing tools.

But there's one additional thing that really made the program work; localized database management. I discovered that the more we did for distributors, the more they wanted us to do for them. This included things like writing the boilerplate customer letters for them and teaching their as yet untrained office staff to use computers.

Our distributors had two factors that contributed to their pushing us for more support:

- The ability to pressure Mega-Flush with the inherent threat of pulling the business
- Unabashed greed. It was far cheaper to have us do this work for them than to devote resources to it themselves.

Herein lies a principle:

- We are taught in school that we need to find products that fill customer needs.
- On the other hand, all business is motivated by greed.
- Therefore, when it comes to satisfying customers' needs, eventually, **Greed Replaces Need.**

I saw an opportunity here. And so, with the relative level of altruism typical those days of Corporate America, I recommended developing a simple database program that we could administer for our distributors. This would be the key to their marketing programs so that they would be able to manage customer lists, do the direct mails, and then analyze their markets. Top management at Mega-Flush loved it and gave me the go-ahead to develop it.

After testing the software I had written, I offered to set up these programs for distributors on a local basis and teach their office staffs how to use them. As an enticement, Mega-Flush also promised that we would use these databases to support them with national direct mailing programs.

Keep in mind, that we maintained our harmless "we're so glad you're letting us do this for you." persona.

This eagerness on the part of our distributors to use our resources and save money gave us exactly what we were looking for: access to their databases of customers as we set them up in the software. Except for some of the smaller companies that still suffered from a dose of healthy paranoia, few asked for any sort of assurances that we wouldn't send anything to their customers without them knowing it.

Most of the larger distributors didn't seem to think about this. This is because the owners of the larger companies delegated the detail work to people who had little concern about such issues. Most of these middle managers were more interested in the process of keeping their jobs, than why they were actually doing them.

For the majority of the few who raised such issues, Mega-Flush got by with verbal agreements. For the one or two others, our legal department "weasel worded" a simple non-binding letter. It is important to note at this time, that our company president stated that he wanted to create an "aura of trust" with our distributors. Other times, he indicated that he wanted to develop an "environment of trust" for our customers.

At no time did he ever state that he wanted to actually *create* trust between us and our customers. He only wanted to give the impression that we were trustworthy. In his third book, How to Exploit Your Customers' Sense of Trust, Iram Casten teaches us that it is entirely possible to create the "aura of trust" without ever doing anything trustworthy. Further, he warns that a successful company should never actually pursue trustworthiness as it sets a dangerous precedent that is difficult to back away from.

But I digress.

As I had predicted, not only did the program work to increase participating distributors' business in their respective markets, it increased our business with the distributors.

But nothing lasts for very long in business. A year or so down the road many of our distributors took what they had learned from us, as I had also predicted, and used it to sell cheaper products from our competitors. After all, betrayal is the American Way in business.

Many of them now told us that if we came up with more, better and newer programs that we might have a chance to get their business back again.

Having no written agreements with us, these distributors were able to repudiate any assumptions we might have made about their potential loyalty, or implied quid pro quo for using the programs we had developed for them.

And, on the other hand, our salesmen could just as easily repudiate any allegations made by the distributors with regard to the use of customer lists.

But we were prepared for this. I had been learning from our Distributors how to do it to them first. If they complained, at higher levels, everybody, including our CEO could claim complete deniability.

I had made sure that Legal had already laid the groundwork for this turn of events. From Legal's point of view:

All we had agreed to was that we would not send anything to "distributors'" customers without their knowledge. Therefore, if we informed the distributors that we were sending customers mailings, we were well within legal bounds.

Consequently, as distributors broke from the fold, we did send them letters letting them know what we were doing.

Further, due to our lower direct-to-retailer pricing, most of the retail customers rushed to open direct accounts with us. After selling an opening order to any of the companies on these lists directly, we now considered these customers as "our" customers. This revoked the obligation to inform distributors of anything in the future as they were no longer considered customers of the distributors.

Once we had pirated these individual databases, we assigned them to our Direct Sales Division. Next, to ensure continued business with these direct accounts, we gave them even deeper graduated discounting that was roughly equal to the markup charged by distributors. This alone would lock distributors out of their own markets, as there was no margin left for them.

Bottom line: Creating the "aura of trust" with these distributors was a successful marketing tactic. It helped us get proprietary information that enabled us to increase our business.

Final note: Once I had developed these programs for the company, they no longer had a use for me either. But I had sensed this, and had already made other plans. As a concession, at my exit interview, I was awarded an Elwood Birch Lifetime Achievement Golden Bowl award. (See chapter X.)

Exercise:

Now here's a simple test you can perform with a minimum of fuss and bother:

Weasel Factor Quotient (WFQ)

In relationship to actually having to follow through on commitments or promises made to customers or to employees:

_____%	What percentage would be repudiated by your CEO?
_____%	What percentage would be repudiated by your other officers?
_____%	What percentage would be repudiated by your salespeople (Assume a base for sales of at least 75%)
_____%	What percentage would you repudiate?
_____%	Total up the above and divide by four. (**Your WFQ**)

This is where you rank in relationship to other companies

WFQMeaning

87%-98%*	Congratulations, your company ranks with the top 100 Corporations in America.
77%-86%	Doing well, you're in with the top 500 Corporations in America.
50%-76%	You are on a par with the top 2000 Corporations in America.
25%-49%	To get on a par with the 2000 Corporations, you need significant improvement.
0%-24%	You rank with most small companies.

*It is never possible to get a 100% WFQ rating.

There are still those individuals in corporations who believe in personal integrity. This is the absolute antithesis of the Weasel Factor Quotient and will undermine an otherwise sound business. Therefore, until these people are completely eliminated, no perfect WFQ score will ever be possible.

Rose's Rule of Business #3: **Trust is one-sided, not reciprocal**

Anything a company does in relationship to building trust with a customer, no matter how "customer-focused" it may seem, has only one purpose: To extract additional money from the customer in one manner or another for its own benefit. And once one of your employees has accomplished this for you, his or her usefulness to you is at an end.

VII. Growing Short-Term Profits Without Growing Gross Sales
CASE STUDY 4: Mega-Flake Corporation

When building a marketing organization, companies make a lot of noise about long-term strategic planning and growth. They talk about "growing the organization." They tell employees things like...

"We promote from within."
"You are our biggest resource."
"We value experience."
"We value loyalty and will reward it."

Sound familiar? But when a company fails to make a profit that is as large as expected in any quarter, what happens?

- The stock goes down.
- There are board meetings.
- Blame is assigned.
- Quick fixes are sought.
- Whether or not fixes are found, people are fired or reassigned.
- New programs are developed, no matter how lame.
- East Coast consultants are brought in.
- More process is put in place.

The analogy I have drawn from this is that *business is the ultimate bratty child in search of a tantrum*. This is human nature. Our society is self-focused and business reflects these values. So why not use it to your advantage?

Hard work is only rewarded insofar as it is convenient for the company. It's the old analogy of the locomotive pulling the freight cars. In business, the people who do the actual work collectively are the locomotive pulling the freight cars, or profits. Once you get the cars to where you want them, you can disconnect the locomotive. You only need it again when you want to get the cars moving once more. This is why large companies are constantly staffing up and down.

But I digress.

Mega-Flake, the giant milling company in a major metropolitan market had been profitable for decades. In the early eighties, due to general market sluggishness, dividends flattened out temporarily. In addition, Mega-Flake's president, a long-term builder, took a large write-down and put a huge amount back into upgrading facilities to help posture for the future. This was a stupid thing to do, but he was under the impression that he still had a career.

Whatever.

Rochelle Marks and I had worked together for a short time in the sixties and had remained friends ever since. When her husband died, Rochelle had gone back to work and had been with Mega-Flake for about sixteen years at this time.

She was product manager of Godawful's Pizzas, a company in Mega-Flake's subsidiary, Cheap Gut Stuffer Foods, Inc. Part of her responsibilities were to keep finding substitutes in the manufacture of the product to keep it competitive with the competition's gut-stuffer pizzas, and make it more profitable.

Her years of superlative performance were based upon her refined rationalizations on how cheapening the product actually made it better. Rochelle was one of the best at this that I had ever known. Her euphemistic explanations not only founded the basis of the copy platforms on which all advertising was built, but the business plans she presented to top management carried this to a fine art.

This was, in fact, what was expected, and she regularly demonstrated this expertise to her bosses. It had gained her a certain reputation within the company. "No one develops and manages Bullshit like Rochelle does." it was often remarked. Thus, she had been promised, at one point to be made the next group product manager of their Total Crap Foods Division.

The same year, the analysts started pushing technology stocks, and holders of Mega-Flake began dumping stock. The board got upset and reacted by firing the president who had stupidly invested so much in their future.

In keeping with the trends of the decade the board formed a search committee. The new CEO, an MBA from Kellogg, "walked the walk, talked the talk." This next wave of business geniuses were polished, educated con-men, who had gone to prestigious schools to refine their shell games. This one was as good as the rest at finagling and manipulating spreadsheets, cash-flow, and other tools at his disposal to make his activities look dramatic to an impressionable public and board of directors.

The "Organizing for Growth" campaign he introduced was a masterful plan to lay off about 1200 people during the next twelve months and "convince" another three hundred to "voluntarily" leave. Several of the less immediately profitable subsidiaries were also targeted for sell off.

In most cases, the companies that bought these subsidiaries had mistakenly maintained a longer term perspective. They believed that these business units had great potential for large profits if they were just given a few years to develop. Consequently, they were willing to risk the downside of not having immediate profits from these acquisitions.

Talk about stupid.

In addition, this CEO developed his own heroic corollary to "Just-in-time manufacturing." He figured, "What the heck, if we can squeeze blood out of our suppliers, how about doing it to our customers, too?"

It was more than clever. The enticement to the customers was that they could, through means of automated inventory with hand-held scanners, and their own mainframe computers, "modem" orders via telephone tie-line to Mega-Flake. Once they had these customers tied in, it was a simple means of using the same ordering information to instantly generate bills before the merchandise was even shipped. That year, the Board rewarded him for his coup with a bronzed replica of a millstone.

Mega-Flake also went from 2% 10 days, to a 2% cash basis, or Net 10 days. This essentially meant that these customers would have to pay for the order up-front in order to get their usual 2% discount.

Internally, the CEO called it "Just-In-Time Cash" but gave it the external name of "Instant Access Ordering" to make it sound good to customers. In truth, it was "Instant Access Billing." This was the best example of the axiomatic "Get the Money First" concept I had ever seen.

Naturally, this innovative concept made him a lot of friends with other CEO's who copied his program. But on the other hand, grocers also knew how to take care of themselves, and just upped their chargebacks to Mega-Flake for hidden damage and broken bag or broken box credits.

Read "Vacationing On Your Suppliers' Float," by Vituccio Levine, The Grocer's Chargeback Monthly, January 1984, for a complete listing of common invoice deductions you can use with your suppliers. This landmark article started a groundswell of activity in the grocery trade.

In retaliation, Mega-Flake introduced a new dealer load incentive program to counter. This was nothing more than the old "20 up 10 down" scheme. This was first introduced by Warren Wm Stein as the "Grocer's Irritation Factor Discount." In 1923. It was based upon the principle that you must first jack the price up by 20% in order to give them a 10% discount. The additional 10% is to compensate you for just having to do business with them in the first place.

A year later, the company, with about twelve percent less in revenues, but an eighteen percent net increase in earnings, and now cash-rich, saw their stock price increase. According to a number of stock analysts, Mega-Flake had "eliminated excesses, and effected many new synergies..." and therefore upgraded the stock from a "sell" to a "hold."

Nevertheless, the new CEO, cashed in his options at the end of the second year. He'd accomplished his goal...*getting rich beyond his wildest dreams.*

Not long after, however, some of the short-term actions began catching up with Mega-Flake. Earnings, revenues and stock all came crashing down. This resulted in further layoffs of another 800 people, including the CEO. By then, it didn't matter to him.

The third year, the company, now much smaller, and down approximately 10 notches on the Fortune 1000, was acquired by a foreign firm for approximately 65% of what its value had been four short years earlier.

Remember, while ignoring irrelevant business concerns for the long-term this generated a few more cents per share in the short term which enabled the CEO to achieve his secondary personal goal of again doubling that which he had already pillaged.

At this point, Rochelle, my old acquaintance contacted me and asked if I could help her out. She was four months short of being fully vested to receive a deferred retirement of approximately $550 a month, when she retired at age 62, in another fifteen years. She had two children in high school and one in college at the time.

She had begged not to be laid off with only one-hundred and twenty days remaining until her pension was assured. She said she'd be glad to take a demotion, work as a cleaning person, anything.

Justifiably so, there was no yielding on the part of Mega-Flake's HR (hiring and removing) department. Policy was policy. They simply didn't need any more superfluous people at this time and it would only incur a long-term obligation that they didn't want to pay.

It wasn't really that difficult to understand. There were two-hundred and eighty-seven people in this category, with less than a year to go before being totally vested in the retirement plan. By removing them from the payroll, Mega-Flake eliminated a good deal of long-term debt, and thus made themselves very attractive for a takeover or buy-out by another company.

Obviously, I couldn't do anything for Rochelle. She had let herself become one of the little people and really couldn't do anything for me that a thousand other people could do a lot cheaper. After all, business is business.

Despite losing her house, a lengthy convalescence after back surgery, and being evicted from two apartments, Mega-Flake had never forgotten Rochelle. Their dogged determination to keep her on their newsletter mailing list made it possible for her to keep abreast of those within the company who had been promoted, gone on vacations, won awards and retired. More importantly, it kept them in contact with her when they were ready to exploit her talents further.

A year after the takeover, when the new owners needed to hitch the locomotive on again, they offered her and a hundred or so others their old jobs back at half salary. This saved the company millions in salary and millions in benefits that it no longer had to pay.

Rose's Rule of Business #4: In Business, there is no "Long Term"

Growth in Business is all short-term profits. Therefore, your only concern is for the appearance of Growth for the company so that you can grow your own bank account.

VIII. Can You Really Afford to Be Civilized in Business?
Our Basic Nature

This chapter is pretty simple: We're all basically savages. The World is a rough place. Sure, we've come out of the literal jungle, but we still live in a virtual one. And we venture out into it at an early age.

We're divided into predators and prey. This begins in grade school and we should get better at identifying who is which.

I learned in school, that we are either afraid of being bullied, and losing our color crayons, or getting punched out, or others are afraid of us.

When I was five years old, I played together frequently with my classmate, Billy Boogerman. He was twice my size. One day when we were playing, with absolutely no provocation on my part, Billy punched me in the nose, bloodying it. I went home crying.

"Why are you bleeding?" my mother asked. "It's stupid and you're making a mess." (I'd indicated earlier, that my mother was not typical.)

I told her why. She gave me two pieces of Kleenex and told me to use the garden hose outside.

When my father got home and told my mother what she should have done, they both told me "Go and punch him back."

I didn't get it. I was afraid. But at this point, I was more afraid of them, than him. So I marched back to his house, confronted him and took a swing at his face. He blocked the blow, deflecting it. I connected with his neck instead and knew I'd caused him pain. He retaliated by knocking me on my rear-end. It didn't hurt and somehow, I felt better and then promptly proceeded to forget about the whole incident.

Some time later I was playing with another friend, Eugene Yapperstein. Gene was my size, but slighter in build. He was the male equivalent of a "Chatty Cathy." One day, in the middle of one of his lectures, I felt the sudden urge to do to him what Billy had done to me.

You're probably thinking that I realized it was wrong and withheld the urge. Right?

Nose bloodied, Gene went home crying to his parents.

I had learned the following important lessons that week.

- No matter how safe you think you are, you are never far from a bloody nose. Billy had been my best friend. So much for the longevity of that relationship.
- If you play with the big boys, sometimes there can be big consequences. It's better to start off with someone nearer your own size.
- Shit flows downhill. Make sure you're uphill.
- If you're attacked, fight back. You might not be successful, but you won't feel like a putz.

- Bleeding is stupid and messy.

On the second point, I'm not saying that I didn't feel remorse over hitting Gene. But I got over it.

I never got that close to Billy Boogerman again. From then on, I always looked for danger signs before making friends and decided that I would only befriend those I could bully.

Later in life, I learned that business is all bullies and bloody noses.

As we get older, most of us learn that physical violence is not productive, so we learn whatever it is that is necessary to avoid it, but still be successful and intimidating other people.

In the next three chapters I'll explain how, by understanding your fears and accommodating them you can learn critical bullying skills. These will help you work the system to your benefit so that you can be successful.

Exercise:

In relation to your fears about the workplace and your true motivation for working, which best describes your waking thoughts? Which of these should it be?

- "My colleagues at Mega-Barf are real geniuses. Therefore, I'll do anything they ask, because I know they are right, not because I need the job or because I fear reprisal if I don't."
- "I feel so secure in my job at Mega-Purge, my world revolves around the company's suppositories. I'm not the

least embarrassed by what the company produces.

- "I would never compete unfairly just to ensure my own job security. I'd rather be terminated while doing business honestly than be employed as a result of my deceit.
- "A bad day working is better than a good day golfing."
- "How am I going to justify my phony-baloney product with declining market-share one more day so that I can continue to support my family?"
- "Who can I climb over or bully to get ahead."

Rose's Rule of Business #5: Being the bully is better than being bullied.

We are all savages. We only think we are civilized. As we mature, we simply get better at justifying our savagery and find ways to make bullying more effective and more subtle. These skills are the basis of Corporate America's culture.

IX. True Subjectivity Requires Creativity

The corollary skill to intimidation is subversion. Billy Boogerman and I stayed in the same class until we were in the third grade, when he got sent to Leavenworth for racketeering. But I took on a whole new attitude after our brief altercation. First, I looked for someone else in the class that was as big as Billy. I sized up Wayne "Hutch" Hutchinson, and eventually decided that he was probably as tough as Billy, but perhaps a little easier to read.

Even at five years old, Hutch was good-looking. He was tall, blond, muscular, talked in sports metaphors, had light blue eyes, a cleft chin and a neck somewhat wider than his head.

But I digress.

Hutch was good at kick ball, and I was good at letters, numbers and wisecracks. We formed a friendship. I stuck with him at kick ball, while he learned letters, numbers and how to be a smartass from me. I made sure I walked to and from school with him.

I could now be subjective enough to tell myself that I wasn't really afraid of Billy anyway. This is due to what I call the concept of "Creative Reality."

What is the difference, you may ask between plain old "Subjective Reality" and "Creative Reality." It's simple. Subjective Reality can be positive, negative or neutral. When you add the "Creative" part, it becomes a tool. You make it positive and eliminate any possibility of negativity and use it to create momentum to help you solve something.

This is what I was doing when I told myself that I wasn't really afraid of Billy anymore. Eventually, I didn't think about him, except for the days that Hutch was sick and didn't accompany me to school. Then, I kept looking over my shoulder. But I was sure it wasn't because I was afraid of Billy. You see, I had begun to actually believe my "Creative Reality" and it gave me a better feeling about myself. This really helped me throughout my life allowing me to become a CEO. Once I had reached that goal, I could much more easily start believing my own Bullshit press, which had been carefully crafted by my Bullshit writers.

Therefore, over the course of my life I've used my Creative Reality to maintain my momentum.

You see, when most people are in a job they are not just afraid of getting a bloody nose. They are afraid of losing their homes and not being able to support their families. This is because a bully in business can take away their livelihood.

So "fear of failure," replaces "fear of bloody nose."

But the fear of failure doesn't end with just being able to survive. Even those who are more affluent or financially secure are afraid of failure by way of losing status.

The corporation VP is afraid that he'll lose his job and will only be able to get a lesser one.

The CEO who is a patron of the arts is afraid her name won't appear at the top of the patron's list.

The commanding general is afraid of screwing up when the war comes on his watch. Or if he wins it, he is afraid that it will not be nearly well enough for the press pundits or his critics.

The Nobel Laureate is afraid that someone else's work will eclipse his own.

The power broker is afraid her base of influential friends will slip away from her.

I saw this as early as junior high school. There were the tough guys, the really smart ones, and those, particularly from the rich families, who were already power brokers. Me, I was just working hard to keep my head above water.

And in my early years, I felt terribly inadequate because of my limitations. I didn't understand how I would survive. How could I be tougher, smarter, more powerful? Most of them were already way ahead of me.

The truth was that I couldn't possibly compete with people who had advantages that I didn't have. There was no way I could re-write my genetic code and then be born taller, smarter, better-looking, or be born into a richer family.

So I had to find my niche somewhere else. I realized at an early age, that I would probably not have the kind of life they or their parents had. But I was determined to find my place, and make it as good as I was able.

The times I had visited with my friends who were better off, there was a kind of "noblesse oblige" attitude about it. In today's terms, I was the disadvantaged kid from the other side of town. We ate tuna fish and they ate steak.

At one of those visits, a passage from a Dickensian novel came to mind. I was being granted crumbs from the rich men's tables. It stuck with me. And I resented being in that position.

But this still wasn't going to stop me from trying to maximize what I had.

Then human nature took over and I began telling myself another story. Much of the ground work had already been laid by my father. Rationalization was another one of his great strengths. And rationalization is the beginning of "Creative Reality."

So I began telling myself that none of it mattered. I didn't necessarily have to compete with them. What I had to do was be successful at getting what I wanted from them. In order to do this, I had to know what their weaknesses were.

After that, the rest was simple. I could use intimidation, fear, misdirection, bald-faced lies, white lies, destructive lies, lies of betrayal and a whole lot more. More about that in later chapters.

The lesson I had learned here was that there's an angle for almost any situation you find yourself in. All you have to do is create the right perception. This generally takes a healthy dose of "Creative Reality" to do it.

Exercise:
List three things you did at work this week associated with the use of Creative Reality.

Rose's Rule of Business #6: Bullying is not an exact science, but rather a creative art.
From birth, most conscious activities are focused on dealing with our fears and inadequacies. To start your training as a CEO, you must determine how best to use these feelings in others in order to successfully bully them.

X. Worming Your Way Into The Organization Through Creative Reality

Once we understand them, we can learn to accommodate our fears. After all, pandering is one of the most developed of human traits, so why not pander to ourselves? We all want to be recognized and feel important. So we scramble with whatever we have to get to wherever it is we are eventually going. Unfortunately, most of us never get to where we really want to be, like this guy in an old obituary I stumbled across in 1966. It stuck with me, because I knew I didn't want to wind up like him.

> *"Elwood Birch, executive Vice President For Research On Piece-Parts Redesign Of Hinges for Personal Products Technologies, Inc. died at home Saturday, of natural causes at the age of fifty-six.*
>
> *Birch, will be best remembered by the industry he served faithfully for twenty-seven years, as the developer of the single-rivet design for attaching hinges to the body of the Zephyr, Personal Products' revolutionary personal banquette. The improvement significantly brought costs down, making the Zephyr toilet seat affordable for millions of families, as well as being attachable to personal commodes from a large variety of toilet manufacturers.*
>
> *On his deathbed, Birch was heard to say. `I only wish I had spent more time at work'."*

The plumbing industry's Consolidated Researchers for Applied Products-Institute of Technology (CRAP-IT) has honored Birch by establishing the Elwood Birch Lifetime Achievement Golden Bowl award. It will be granted annually to that individual who best typifies promoting the use of technology in the furtherance of bodily functions."

I've known lots of people who started out to be educators, doctors, engineers, or aviators. Unfortunately, many of those same people wind up winning awards for "Excellence" in selling aftermarket lawn tractor accessories. You can induce, however, from this, that it's not the love of the job that typically drives us. It is, once again the fear of failure.

Large organizations worship at this altar. Most of us, myself included, will typically embrace the litany as well as the liturgy of this church. We learn early to obey the dogma and show the proper respect for its icons.

For many of my generation, this started in the military, when compulsory service was still mandated for males above the age of eighteen.

Identify The Dominant Culture (The Religion Practiced)

Consequently, the United States Air Force was my first large organization. This is the first place I ever experienced what was later called "Corporate Culture" in the private sector.

I will discuss Corporate Culture in a separate Chapter. This is tantamount to organized religion.

Several months before my anticipated promotion to first lieutenant, my commanding officer, a senior captain, was relieved of command and summarily dismissed from the Air Force. This was the modern equivalent of a human sacrifice at the fear of failure altar. This did not bode well for any of his former subordinates in our squadron. We were all potential sacrifices.

We learned, just prior to Thanksgiving, that we were to have a new commander, an experienced major who was a "mustang," i.e., a former enlisted man who had risen through the ranks to become an officer.

He had also been a p.o.w. during "the Big One". At that time, he'd been a young enlisted radio operator on a B-17, and had been shot down over Italy. He'd spent sixteen months in a German P.O.W. camp prior to the end of the war in Europe.

And, I was to be his sponsor, meaning that it was my job to arrange for housing, administrative services, prepare his office, and so forth in advance of his arrival. I communicated with him via AUTODIN, which was an early military precursor of Internet, prior to his arrival. I indicated what I had already done and asked what else he might need.

"Nothing," had been the terse reply, followed by "Will be arriving by car, sometime after midnight, day after tomorrow, please stay by the phone so that I can get directions to squadron headquarters."

So I fearfully awaited his arrival.

At two a.m., on the day of his arrival, he called and told me he was on the outskirts of town. I drove out to meet him and he followed me back to the installation. He was quite grateful and gracious.

Once out of the car, I got my first good look Major Randall Hardin. He was about my height, 5' 8", dark complected, with two rough scars on his face, and a gravelly sounding voice. He was wearing civvies. He was about my dad's age, mid-forties. There was also no mistaking that this guy was hard as nails.

"Well, kid." he said. "Gotta get some breakfast. Can we get into the day room this time of night? That is, if it has vending machines." he asked referring to the squadron's enlisted men's' lounge.

"Yes, it does, and I've got a set of keys." I replied. "But there are some all night places near the base where we can eat." I suggested a couple, but he insisted on the day room in the interest of saving time.

So we stopped in at the squadron day room. I'd never paid much attention to the vending machines there and had assumed he would grab a couple of candy bars.

Instead, he found one of the machines that had canned food, put in a quarter and got a can of spaghetti. (At that time, a McDonald's hamburger cost 18 cents. He opened the can and ate it at room temperature. I looked surprised and must have shown it.

"Compared to some of the stuff I ate in a P.O.W. camp, this is pretty good." he said by way of explanation. Despite his gruff-sounding voice and hard-bitten face, he had a kind demeanor that put me at ease. I knew I was going to like him.

"So tell me what's screwed up here, kid. Colonel Douglas at Headquarters tells me I got a lot of cleaning up to do."

This was true, the captain Major Hardin was replacing had not only been a terrible administrator, but had actually been fired for a breach of security. Major Hardin, in contrast, inspired confidence, and I began to tell him, without betraying any trusts, what I felt were the strengths and weaknesses of the squadron, and how we could improve. We talked for about two hours as I took him on a tour of the installation.

After touring the AUTODIN Computer Center, the jewel of the base, our last stop was the Base Communications Center, a pit. This was a critical but unglamorous facility, and a real contrast to AUTODIN which was my current assignment.

The Communications Center, had been the straw that had broken Central Region Commander's back as far as the dismissed captain had been concerned. It operated poorly, was constantly cited for technical, communications protocol, and security violations, and was an embarrassment to Regional Command Headquarters. For lack of a captain to fill the position, a senior first lieutenant had been placed in command of the Comm Center. He, too, had been relieved at the same time the captain had, but had been reassigned instead of being cashiered. I felt sorry for the next poor son-of-a-bitch who was given command of the facility.

When we finished the tour, I accompanied Major Hardin back to his office. He took his bag with him into the locker room and exited a few minutes later in dress blues. He looked as if he'd been poured into them. Among the four rows of decorations on his chest were a bronze star, a silver star and a purple heart with an oak leaf cluster. He was now ready to meet the rest of the squadron. It was five, forty-five a.m.

Days later, after he'd had a chance to determine the personal strengths and weakness of his staff, and made a list of things that needed to be done, Major Hardin began holding individual meetings with his officers.

I'd gotten to know him a little bit by then, and thought he might be amenable to listening to me. I thought I had a pretty good idea of what was coming next. By then he'd made a couple of reassignments. I would undoubtedly be moved within the organization. I also knew that one of the remaining captains in the squadron would be given command of the dreaded Base Communications Center. My one fear was that I not be assigned as this poor captain's executive officer, as it would, no doubt, be the end of my short career. But I did want to stay in AUTODIN, and hoped I might parlay this into a chance at advanced programmer's school.

On the other hand, I had a cousin who was doing well selling corrugated silos to farmers on government-subsidized parity programs. He said there was always room for me in rural Georgia were I to unexpectedly leave the Air Force with a note home to my mother.

Once seated in Major Hardin's office, I began to speak. But before I could utter a word, the Major did.

"I know, Jonah. You'd like the Base Communications Center. You've got it." he began and handed me a sheet of paper.

It was hard not to vomit.

Accept The Dogma, Religious Confirmation

Just in case I was unclear, I did not want the Base Comm Center. In that brief instant, I replayed my conversations with Major Hardin. I was sure I had never given him any indication that I'd wanted anything to do with it.

The whole idea went against my grain. I wanted to bolt. But before the shock could set in, I read his face. Did he think he was doing me a favor? It didn't seem like it. Nor did it seem that this point was negotiable. So I decided for the time being to keep my big mouth shut and just listen to what my squadron commander had to say. This proved to be a smart move, and formed the basis of another lesson in my mind.

"We've got our work cut out for us, Jonah." he said. "You've got low morale there, because you have people in the wrong jobs, qualified people who are overdue for promotions, and a dingy facility to boot.   Start changing some of those things, and the performance will get a lot better. Here are some things that'll help you get started." he said, handing me a list. "I don't expect that you'll turn that place around overnight, but in six months it should be doing at least an adequate job."

Not only had he done the hard part by mapping out what needed to be done, he'd passed over two captains to give me the job. He obviously wanted me to succeed and had given me the tools to do it without setting an unrealistic expectation.   But if I kept my mouth shut now, my worst fear of being associated with this unglamorous facility would be realized. My ego was at stake here.

So I had to weigh which would be worse; taking the assignment or attempting to turn it down, (assuming I even had the option.)

I reasoned that Major Hardin was already on my side. He wanted me to succeed, and would probably put at my disposal, the tools to get the job done. If I was successful, I'd really get on his good side. If I had trouble, he'd help me.

But utter one word indicating my unwillingness, and there was no telling how it might affect my career. So I opted to prostitute my mediocrity, swallow my ego and appear to gladly take on this assignment. This, too, proved to be a smart move.

Initially, I hadn't gotten the point. Why had he placed me, a second lieutenant, in charge of this facility? After I had a chance to reflect, I realized that Major Hardin was plenty cagey. My initial assessment of his toughness was right. He'd done this before, and knew exactly what he was doing.

He had placed his established "deacons," the senior captains of the squadron, in "safe" places to ensure their loyalty, and placed me, who had little to lose and everything to gain in the place of highest risk.

This was smack in the middle of the altar of the fear of failure.

If I faltered, it could be blamed on youth or inexperience. If I succeeded, I'd be a superstar and would have the Major to thank.

It all made sense. Except for the shit I'd have to take from the other guys.

At first, my fellow second lieutenants kidded me about "sucking hind tit." I, on the other hand, professed that I was willing to put my personal goals behind that of the squadron's, and that I had been given a great (read holy) opportunity to be of service. Thus I had begun to pander to myself and start to develop my own Creative Reality. It hadn't been my initial intent to suck up to the Major, but rather, put it in the light of doing what was right for the overall good of the Squadron, and that somebody had to do it.

Again, I digress.

If all this bullshit is making you sick, take a short break. It was all standard Air Force "party line," a religion unto itself. My peers didn't believe it either, but had expected that this is what I would have said. Even I didn't believe a word of it. But we all sang the same hymns. I was just posturing. And it shut the rest of them up. They grudgingly granted that while I may be a chump, at least I wasn't a complainer. I could live with that.

Ultimately I worked my butt off to carry out the instructions Major Hardin had given me, and in so doing, learned how you get things done in a large organization. Not the least of this, was learning who the Air Force gods really were. I'd learned the litany. Success or failure was not so important as falling in line, suborning myself to the hierarchy, and keeping in lock-step discipline.

The discipline, I next learned, was what I really needed to carry out my program. This included more than just hard work and passing the litany downward to my NCO's and Airmen. It also involved the relentless use of other tools at my disposal; lying, cheating, and stealing. I would realize later, that these qualities would serve me well in Corporate America.

Major Hardin assigned a seasoned staff sergeant, Harry Hamhander to help me write bogus reports about how bad things were so we could show improvement later when we applied the solutions we'd already developed. Command loved the track record this demonstrated as it coincided with a fledgling quality program called "Zero Defects." The Air Force did this twenty years before Corporate America ever thought of doing it. Later I learned, this had set the stage for similar programs in business.

In changing the perception of the Base Comm Center, the people who worked there began to actually believe that things had changed. They hadn't, other than getting a coat of paint on the walls, cleaning the light fixtures, moving some equipment around and relaxing the work and break schedules so that things were more pleasant for the people who worked there. But it was a start.

Become a "Deacon"

Three months later, I'd promoted two of my airmen who were long overdue for promotion based on their contributions, finished the physical cleanup of the facility and instituted new message checking policies.

We'd gone from the Central Region cellar to having the third fewest citations in the region. So, while we were not quite at the top of the region's list, we were on our way, and we were only halfway through the six months. It was, as a coincidence, the month I pinned on my first lieutenant's bars. A year later, we were winning excellence awards, and were asked to share our procedures with other Comm Stations in Central Region. This was their attempt at "putting process in place" or "re-engineering the organization" as it was called some twenty years later in Corporate America.

Although he'd just been "working me" at the beginning, by then, Major Hardin had become like a second father to me. As hardened as he was on the outside, and mischievously devious on the inside, there was a real decency and honesty to his character that used to be common among our leaders. Unfortunately, I learned later that these qualities, while thriving in the Service, had little to do with civilian life. When he was promoted to Lieutenant Colonel, my name was placed on the Captain's List, two years ahead of schedule and I was given a prime assignment to Tokyo.

Having mediocre talents at best, I had slipped through the cracks as a "superstar" just by singing louder than anybody else in the choir. I was well on my way.

Our successes had gladdened Colonel Hardin. "Here's another dirty deal we've gotten into together," he would say good-naturedly and wink when we started a new project.

But the part of this that I liked, was my sense of belonging. Colonel Hardin was a little unorthodox in some of his methods, but some of the most successful people I have met since, were also unorthodox.

Substantively, Corporate America converts the employee to worship Corporate Culture the same as the military, but unlike the Air Force, there is no base of morals, sincerity or personal integrity. Although corporations try feigning these qualities, it is just eyewash and one needs to know how to play at them without really developing them. With Corporate America it's only the perception that counts.

The difference in Corporate America, once I learned this, was that I needn't do the kind of all out job I had in the Air Force, just appear as if I had. So once you've been converted and worship as you are supposed to, you're given the benefit of the doubt. Things are made easy for you to go along. If you make a big show of your piety, success will usually come with it regardless of how mediocre a job you do.

Exercise:

Here's a simple test to _determine just how far you are willing to go_ to pursue your own survival within an organization. Then, when you have achieved CEO-dom, _you should expect this from your underlings._

This is one of the rare areas where it is necessary to grade yourself honestly. Only then will you have a true measure of yourself. Under T/F, score ten points for each true answer, zero for false.

I would be willing to...

T/F	
____	Worship the organization's deity as the one and true deity.
____	Forsake the icons of any organization except my current one as false.
____	Speak the name of this deity with reverence in all things
____	Observe the holy days of the organization and keep them sacred
____	Honor the saints of the organization as I would my father and mother
____	Commit human sacrifices for the organization
____	Commit adultery for the organization
____	Commit theft for the organization
____	Give false testimony to further the organization's goals
____	Take the property or even the spouse of my neighbor
	--
____	Total

Your ranking:	
80-100	Excellent, your organizational skills rank you as top-notch.
60-80	Good, but you need more flexibility in order to play in the Fortune 500.
40-60	Only fair, are you really committed to playing in Corporate America?
Under 40	You are not likely to survive in Corporate America.

Rose's Rule of Business #7: Make Sure of How Others Perceive You.

No matter how "gung ho" your efforts seem to your superiors, they have only one purpose; to create the illusion that you are the most pious of the congregation. You can do this by creating your own Creative Reality and getting others to buy into it. Therefore, receive holy communion if offered, accept any and all aid or credit that accrues to you, but don't waste effort doing more than is necessary to perpetuate this myth. When you have gotten to the top, make sure your underlings exhibit these traits.

XI. Subverting The System To Benefit Your Own Selfish Needs

At this point, I feel that I should probably say a word or two about how we market ourselves. After all, this is where it all starts, when we begin stepping on people to start ascending the corporate ladder. But we need to create the perception that we have at least some of the skills to be hired in the first place.

I always keep about two or three types of resumes handy. If necessary, I'm sure I could generate dozens. I keep track of which one I send in response to a possible job opening so that I can remember what I've said, and to whom. But there's another good reason for that. Once personnel directors see your name in conjunction with a term such as "Manufacturing" or "Marketing" they will never get it out of their heads that you may have other talents than that one narrow function.

But your resume is only a snapshot in time. My premise here is that the individual is flexible. Although some have more of a tendency towards one type of behavior, given the right opportunity, we can all fill a variety of roles.

Therefore, I determine first, what it is I am looking for and then tailor my cover letter and resume to that particular function. For example:

As an Engineer

When I applied for an engineering position, I used the resume that said "Objective: Senior level position in Engineering Project Management." This pigeon-holed me in their minds already.

As a Marketer Guy
If I was applying for a marketing job, I used the resume that said "Objective: Senior level position in Marketing Management." This directed me to another pigeon hole.

As a Salesperson
But if they already had my engineering or marketing resume and had an opening for a sales manager, I was screwed. I had experience in all of these areas. But since my resume began with marketing, I'm forever a marketing guy in the personnel director's mind. And even though the sales manager experience is listed on the resume, it is doubtful the personnel director will ever weed through it. So you should stick to one or two interchangeable careers once you start moving up.

As a Generalist
What I'd really wanted them to see is that I had skill sets in all three areas. So why were they so narrow-versioned? It is because there are thousands of psychologists, business analysts and others continually trying to quantify human behavior. In so doing they categorize people in whatever arcane system they happen to have developed themselves, or happens to be popular at the time. But that doesn't mean it's true.

So how can you possibly be a viable candidate for more than one type of job?

There are those of you who are now reading this and answering "It's not possible to be considered for more than one kind of position.

These systems are all well-documented, and are legitimate. Personnel directors *are* the accepted wisdom, and they say that one person cannot possibly have two or more different capacities. There must be scientific data to back this up. After all, didn't they just tell me that according to my Meyers-Briggs test I should be a mortician?"

Yeah, sure! Well just in case you are inclined to believe all of today's psychobabble as being scientific, consider this:

When Franz Gall, a German doctor introduced the "scientific" discipline of Phrenology in the early eighteen hundreds as a means of categorizing people, many rushed to adopt it. And for over fifty years, this was the accepted wisdom. It took over a hundred years before common sense won out over quasi-medical Bullshit.

So, Can HR Help You?

In a word, "no." Keep in mind, that while some HR people are good at what they do, the majority have little to do with finding talent, helping other people or understanding the dynamics of the market. Currently, there is a groundswell among the general population in support of legislation that would make it illegal for HR people to breed.

So if I am to be successful in communicating my variety of skills to the proper persons, I have to ensure that I have their attention. In order to do that I must tailor everything I've ever done, including my marketing functions, towards the applicability these attributes might demonstrate with regards to sales. I highly recommend **Credible Dissembling When the Whole Truth Won't Do - A Twenty-First Century Guide to Resume Writing** by Werner Updahl.

Which Type Are You?
Since I truly believe in the flexibility of the individual, and do not subscribe to the hard-and-fast rules as laid down by these modern-day Galls, I would rather describe just a few types of roles people play in organizations in order to successfully promote their skills to survive. Forget about Meyers-Briggs. The following is by no means all-inclusive, and I invite you to mentally search for your own examples.

The Empty Suit
This is the guy who is all form and no substance. We all know this guy. I've played this role myself earlier in my career and now play it in my role as CEO. Consequently, it's one of my favorites. There really isn't anything there, but we sure look good.

Insofar as the organization is concerned, we've never had an original thought. Instead, we take them from one department to another and mix them up in our heads, until we have what we think is something that has a good sound to it. Once we've done this, we are ready to begin repeating it as if it really means something.

One of the best examples I've seen of an empty suit was during the time when I was working at B.S. Inc. (Remember, Business Synergistics?) His name was Tim Hutchinson "Hutch" Robinson, and he truly fit the part. He was tall, blond, muscular, talked in sports metaphors, had light blue eyes, a cleft chin and a neck somewhat wider than his head. In other words, the perfect selection to represent our company. He was a recent sales hire we'd pirated away from a national telecommunications company.

But I Digress.

My first encounter with Hutch was after he'd graduated from his one-week indoctrination course. He acted as if he knew me. He had an actual customer, A.T. & T. He was working with them, and was trying to put together a presentation.

That's where my group came into it. I should have known Hutch was going to be fun to work with when he scheduled a strategy meeting and pronounced it "Stragety" (like tragedy.)

I later learned that Hutch had gone to school at the Greater Dallas School of Marketing Sciences and Acupuncture. It was right across the grassy knoll from what he referred to as the Texas Book "Suppository."

His idea, which was a synthesis of what he'd heard from the various departments, was to show the customer how B.S. Inc. could perform marketing services for clients.

Since he had his own particular brand of English, I'll place my translations in parentheses. Here's how he stated it:

"I think what we ought need to do with this preparation (presentation) is to show the customer in the center of a six-pointed wheel (star.) Each wheel (point) would have something saying in it (would say something.) The six stars (points) could speak to (talk about) what customers do to help us (we do to help them.) We could do services, communications, sales, travel, catalogues, and..." he struggled for the sixth. "Profit." he finally said. "Well, maybe we'll refrain (rephrase) that one" he added. "I dunno. Anyway, that's the details (basics.) We'll have to flush (flesh) out the basics (details.)

For the next month however, and on an almost daily basis, he modified each of the six points to the degree that every one of them had a dozen or more sub points protruding from the center. It started to look so complex that members of my creative team began affectionately referring to it as the "Aztec Marketing Wheel," and snickered every time Hutch came by.

You get the idea. What impressed me so much, however, was that Hutch really seemed to believe what he was doing had some meaning attached to it. And he did it with such enthusiasm that he sold the customer a $2 Million project. Hutch, however, was an extreme case. Others, simply carry information back and forth between the company and customers, without trying to add to or understand it.

Empty suits may be placed anywhere in an organization, but typically do well in sales.

The Visitor

This is the job-hopper, who typically works in product management, but may work in other areas.

If they work in business development, they typically get involved in a lot of teams, write a lot of reports, do a lot of studies, and come up with a lot of ideas, but no substance. They are all distraction, smoke and mirrors. Many times, this person has taken a "cloned" program with him and has used it any number of places.

Many times, it's not even their program to begin with, but someone else's. They are good at getting the right people to buy into their projects and right before they are expected to produce anything of real value, they jump ship.

One such person I knew worked for the **B**ay **A**rea **R**apid **T**ransit (BART) in San Francisco. Thinking that the concept of Marketing BART was a good concept to begin with, he felt that if it worked in San Francisco, it would work anywhere.

Well, up to a point, he was right. When he moved to Trentonville, the TART was an instant marketing success, and TART became a household word.

He next moved to Harristown, and likewise, HART was successful.

Finally, however, he moved to Fargo, where his cloned program for the **F**argo **A**rea **R**apid **T**ransit met with great resistance from the town council. He moved on, but struck gold again in Dallas with the **D**allas **A**rea **R**apid **T**ransit system.

You can easily recognize this type of person, since they never fully get their offices unpacked. Many of the boxes that came in with them, stay right where they are until they move out a year or two later.

The Producer
Unfortunately, not much is known about the person who performs in this role. To most corporations, they are a non-entity since successful companies have so many of them in sales, marketing, engineering and manufacturing.

In sales, they are the people who year-after-boring-year, keep on increasing their sales by eight, ten, or twelve percent. In marketing, they are the people who year-after-boring year find new markets, increase the old ones and gain competitive market share. In engineering and manufacturing, these are the people who also continue to improve the quality of the product while boringly turning it out more efficiently and developing new follow-on patents. Conventional wisdom from Fortune 500 Top Management tells us that this is because they are a commodity, much like the goods and services they produce, and are typically handled as such. Therefore you will never find them at the top ranks of an organization where the "real" people are. Most CEO's, COO's and CFO's agree that they do not merit much attention.

The Antagonist
This person can be found in a variety of situations, but is usually found in the upper ranks of many organizations. He is cantankerous, confrontational, even when not necessary, and typically irrational. This role is sometimes appropriate for the CEO, or perhaps a vice president's job.

The primary role of this person is to say "no" to everyone who comes across his path, and act as the gatekeeper for whatever corporate holy truth the organization maintains. The antagonist is an intimidator, is usually unreasonable and works from emotion.

Ironically, this person may have at one time, been a producer who morphed into an antagonist and therefore, found himself on the fast CEO track. Those who have observed this phenomenon first-hand report that this track for professional development may happen in one of several ways: By direct contact, having worked for an antagonist, experientially as a secondary reaction to job-related stress, or purposefully by taking MBS or MBA courses.

Decades before I became a CEO, at one job, I developed a very popular piece of special-interest software used by doctors for tracking patients. Many of the doctors would have purchased PC's to run it if our company had them and sold them to run our software. I did some research and learned that it would have been easy for us to have a PC built and private-labeled to our specifications at a very competitive price that would have allowed us a nice profit.

So I proposed our getting into the office PC and bundled software business. Besides a good price on the computer, our initial software package would be "free." We would then sell the upgrades when they were issued, at regular prices, thus assuring us an annuity. It would have been tremendously profitable, and we already had a built-in market crying for them. I conservatively estimated that we could have sold $3 million worth the first year at a $1,125,000 gross profit.

I had gotten the approval of everybody on the executive team, with the exception of the VP of General Services and Administration. Mind you, he had nothing to do with the business units, but one veto was all it took. He vetoed it. When I asked him why, he said "When I was at Compensation Abatement Consultants, we tried PC's and I didn't like them. They're a fad."

The Process-Giver

I need to spend a little more time on this type of person than the others, since there are so many of them. This person typically thinks of herself as an administrator and is all process. The process-giver does a lot of the same things as the antagonist. He or she can intimidate, and be unreasonable and works from emotion, but gives the appearance of reason. They do this by building elaborate systems that justify their actions.

Process-givers are usually senior managers and work for VPs and can be counted on to further the VPs lack of progress on new projects and "keep yesterday alive, yet, one year longer," as well as protect other sacred turf.

Rather than creating wealth, this person is consumed with the idea of finding methods by which to control or micro-manage the smallest of details. The purpose is to finally kill any creativity in the people who work for them, lest any one individual look better than the others. And make no mistake about it, these are usually the people who control organizations and thereby control the producers who create the wealth.

It is precisely this "bean counter" mentality that has taken the morality out of business and has rightly replaced it instead, with a credo that squeezes the last drop of profitability out of every function within a company.

These are the same people who created the idea that all accountability is now considered a function that resides with middle management or below. Remember, it's just business, not personal.

The Process-Givers In Action

I worked for Mega-Barf, a personal products company that made an anti-acid. Bulima Bullard who had been a long-time lab assistant worked there, too.

Bulima came from a family of lifelong bean counters and longed to be one herself, but was a late bloomer. Nevertheless, she wouldn't give up, so during the ten years she was injecting rabbits with poisons, she was also taking online classes to get an MBA. The day after she received her MBA, Mega-Barf made her director of Marketing Services.

In yet another affirmative action program gauged to "balance the organization," they figured "What the heck, injecting lab animals with poisons was a service. And, son-of-gun, the poisons that didn't kill the animals were the new products that could be marketed. So, how far was that really from Marketing Services?" It was a fit.

Since Bulima now controlled all advertising and promotion, she picked up one of the ad journals someone had left lying on one of their desks and read an article. She learned that lots of companies changed agencies on a regular basis. So, as her first official act, she decided that she wanted to change creative agencies.

She developed a process that had worked for manufacturers of building materials that she had adapted from one of her classes. It provided a matrix with which to select a vendor. She enforced this drill on her twelve person creative department, much to their chagrin. These were people, it must be noted, who had a collective experience of over one-hundred years in the creative community. They knew the players, they knew who fit Mega-Barf's business. Nevertheless, Bulima needed to show that she was in charge.

When all was said and done, Bulima's matrix indicated that Hendrix and Kokimoto, a design studio whose specialty was working with manufacturers of aluminum windows and siding was the right creative agency for Mega-Barf. Half-a-million dollars and three bad campaigns later, she reluctantly decided that Hendrix and Kokimoto was no longer appropriate for Mega-Barf, not because she had made a mistake, but because the corporation had made a change in direction.

Since Bulima was now considered senior level management, the accountability for the resultant loss of revenues, loss of visibility and loss of status the company had suffered was transferred to members of her creative team who were promptly fired. As a result, Bulima just kept on getting promoted for her innovative processes, and eventually got "tapped" by top management to institute her processes as the corporate controller. She'd finally gotten her dream. If her name sounds familiar, it should. Bulima has since gone on to write a best-seller herself. "**Your Direct Reports, It All Starts There; A Guide to Passing the Buck Downward**."

As a side note, I once heard Bulima refer in total earnestness to GDP as Gross Domestic Process. This became the accepted wisdom at Mega-Barf.

A decade or so previous to Bulima's taking over as Director of Marketing Services, some Process Giver coined the phrase "MBO." This was a time that was still in the early stages of the development of SLIME (Synergistic Language to Improve and Management Effectiveness) as a language.

At that time, the popular liturgy of the Process-Givers stated that a business was managed one of three ways:

Term in SLIME	Meaning
Management by Exception (**MBE**)	Putting out Brush Fires
Management by Process (**MBP**)	Unnecessary elaborate schemes for even the minutest of tasks that justify the existence of administrators where none are needed
Management by Objective (**MBO**)	Committing to inflated goals and then making it sound like you have achieved them

I have also found that despite others claiming to manage a business by one of the above, there are, in reality three other basic ways of managing a business. I call them "The Three MBF's."

My Term	Example
Management by Fear	"Do it or I'll fire you."
Management by Fiat	"Do it because I say so!"
Management by Family	"Be Creative, but what my wife says, goes!"

Most companies, however have their own variation of these, which I call MBS, Management by Stupidity. These are the most pervasive. Recent proponents of this method have included:

British Petroleum
Bear Stearns
Toyota Motor Company
Goldman Sachs

So despite the inherent limitations of being Process Givers, they have made great contributions to Corporate America.

The Cheerleader

This section would not be complete without a few words about the professional panderer. It's one thing to pander if you create something in the process. This person doesn't create anything, however, but gets on everybody's bandwagon. The more bandwagons, the better. That way, if one person's bandwagon gets to be out of favor, there are several others. This person is seen spending most of his or her time going to meetings, re-processing others' ideas, distributing them, and recruiting neutral parties.

Do not, however confuse this person with the visitor. Whereas the visitor leaves after a while, the cheerleader stays through many purges, taking on protective coloration from any of a variety of sources. Some say cheerleaders have even been known to stay with a building through a change of companies, say for instance, a pipe company going out of business and a cement company moving into it's space. This phenomenon is best chronicled in Cryle Furney's 2007 Best Seller, "**Corporate Cockroaches**." Published by Norgas-Tyvak, Inc.

As a sidebar, this person always manages to wind up reporting directly to the CEO, regardless of employment level.

Now, can you identify any of these previous types where you work? You'd better be able to, because they are the very people you need to intimidate into supporting you on your rise to the top. They will be your temporary allies in many cases that will allow your progress and may be discarded when they have no further usefulness.

Be Flexible!

You may be wondering what is the point of this little dissertation on role types.

People are extremely flexible when faced with extinction, which in this case means making a living.

It is possible for anyone to play more than one type of role in order to avoid extinction.

When faced with decisions about how to earn a living, there is usually more than one choice. Take the one that is the most self-serving even if you are not qualified. It will take months or possibly years for anyone to find out.

Try to appear useful when you are not really doing anything.

Skim along the surface of a corporation. It is easier than you might think if you can intimidate enough people into supporting you.

As for me? Well, at one time or another, I have filled every one of these roles on my way to the top. The empty suit and the panderer were two of my favorites.

Learn to Identify These Types Early!

Besides adapting yourself to be one of these types as needs be, learn to identify them so that you can tap into their weaknesses and exploit them to the maximum.

Exercise

Here are some questions you should ask yourself in order to get a better grasp on role playing and how it affects your job.

- Try and determine how many different roles you play in your job.
- Can you identify others?
- How can you exploit them?
- Can you develop your own?
- If you do, could you develop your own step on the corporate ladder that others would leave alone?
- How do people react to you in these different roles?

- Which role do you think is best protected in case of layoffs?
- Can you become this type?
- Can you get by without actually doing any work in this role, but get paid just the same?
- Which of the three MBF's does your company operate under?
- Get yourself into a position where you control one of those MBF's.

Rose's Rule of Business #8: Chameleons have survived on this planet for over 100 million years.

On your rise to the top, you will typically grow into the role in which you have been cast by exhibiting, but not necessarily developing the types of traits expected in that role. Learn who the others are and use them for stepping stones. Remember surviving in a corporation isn't what you contribute. It's the *perception of what you contribute* that counts.

XII. Synergistic Language to Improve Management Effectiveness(SLIME): Definition of Terms in Corporate America

Before delving into the subject of company cultures, it is important to understand that people in large organizations, which include both business and government, speak a language that sounds a lot like English, but is not. This, in effect, institutionalizes lying, and raises it to a new high, as its own art form.

As I first mentioned I have termed this relatively new tongue SLIME.

SLIME Simplified

Since each organization has their own dialect of SLIME, it is important for the individual to master this before proceeding any further.

For example:

- The term "opportunity" in English means an opening, a chance, or a prospect at positive gain, as in "We have several opportunities for you to turn in your old books for credit towards new ones."
- In some corporations, this same word means deficiency, as in "during your review, you will be made aware of several opportunities to correct your lack of progress."
- And, in some corporations it means imminent disaster, as in "We'd like to discuss with you the opportunity of your pursuing other employment possibilities."

- And so it is in New Corporate America that a different language has developed, with as many dialects as there are corporations. Each then, in effect has developed its own language that must be understood before speaking it. Consequently, there is not enough space here, to devote to the SLIME spoken in any one company. There are, however, some commonalities.

Using Titles Will Help You Lord Over Others

The differences in language become readily apparent when an individual first begins looking for a job. So what are some of the terms used to categorize people? In learning to read the Bullshit, one needs to understand these terms. And since they change frequently, one needs to be very observant so as not to miss the changes.

As humans, we are constantly trying to identify each other. This starts in our earliest years trying to identify boys from girls. (And some even get that wrong, i.e., terms like "alternative disposition" or trying to understand books with titles like "Uncle Daddy's Very Special Live-in Friend, Joel.")

What makes it difficult, is that just when we think we have the players identified, someone goes ahead and changes it. Usually it is for the purpose of making someone feel better about his or her lot in life.

The Innovators

We could start with the simple title of President. Less than two generations ago, this was the highest ranking person in any organization. It certainly still works for our federal government. But somewhere along the way, corporations must have experienced some infighting where more than one person wanted to be the president.

Literature on the subject indicates that it might have first started with organized crime in the fifties and sixties. We are told that several of the crime organizations realized that killing each other wasn't a very sophisticated way of solving problems and sought a way to end the practice.

We don't know for sure, but those who lived it, say it went something like this:

Manny, Jake and Irv all operated separate crime families in the same large Midwestern city. For purposes of money laundering and doing business on a day-to-day basis, each had their own legitimate corporations. Nevertheless, they argued over territories, and periodically killed off large numbers of each other's organizations while neglecting their day-to-day business; extorting money or running numbers.

After a particularly bloody period, several of these dons realized that this was just reducing their revenues. They also realized that by either merging or acquiring one another they could get better prices on accidental assassination insurance, fleets of getaway cars, and business supplies from Smith & Wesson.

In order to do this they needed to form a legitimate corporation with legitimate sounding names and titles. Since each was used to being the chief of their own legitimate organization, through which they were able to launder money and therefore operate somewhat legally, it wasn't going to work to if one of them appeared to have a higher status than the others.   And clearly, they had resolved not to go back to the old ways of shedding blood. So when they began the process of combining their corporations, the bickering over titles had to be avoided before it ever started.

Irv was recognized as their chief-of-chiefs because he was the most insightful and usually the quickest to act. (He was also the meanest son-of-a-bitch of the group.) One evening he had a revelation, and presented it to the group the next day. It was really simple:

"Hey guys," he began, "We can all sound like wheels. One of us'll be the prez, one of us'll call himself the chairman of the board, like that Mayo Say `dung' guy in China and the other can be the Chief Embezzlement Officer like that sumbitch over at General Motors calls himself. Am I makin' sense, or what?"

"Executive Officer." Manny corrected.

"Yeah, sure." Irv said.

"Sounds good." Jake replied.

They all agreed he was making sense and adopted his proposal. And so it was settled.

The Imitators

One day, a number of years later Hans Schwanz, president of Mega-Press, one of the largest publishers of tabloid newspapers in the country was watching a gangster movie, based loosely on the above story. Schwanz liked the idea of the three titles. It just so happened, that he was looking for a way to keep two of his VP's happy so they wouldn't quit. So Mega-Press became the first of the big companies to follow this example. Schwanz promptly promoted the two VP's and ensured their undying commitment, (at least for the next several accounting periods.)

It wasn't long before the rest of the big companies followed suit, and made some of their VP's either presidents or CEO's, while keeping the title of chairman of the board for the real president.

The Adulterators

But as is the case with all good ideas, it got confusing. No sooner did many of these companies adopt this idea, than did some of their real top executives begin to become jealous of their subordinates.

The first recorded incident was in 1987, when Richard Baishik, who was President of the Knollwood Knockwurst Company, decided that he liked the titles of CEO and Chairman of the Board better than President, and wanted them for himself. So he fired his father and mother, and not being able to settle on any one of the titles, decided to become President, CEO and Chairman of the Board.

And so the modern trend was born. And not to be outdone by small companies, when the big corporations heard of this trend, they were quick to lead the market in copying it.

And truly, anyone now, who is the real power in any big organization, isn't worth spit, unless he has all three titles.

But I digress.

In learning to read the Bullshit, it's important to determine what some of these terms or titles really mean. This can be confusing and doesn't apply only to business. I'll give you an example:

"Significant other" is one such "SLIMED" term.   What the hell is it supposed to mean? The first time I heard that, was when my single brother-in-law used it. My reply was, "If it was any real relationship, you'd call that lady your girlfriend, wife, fiancée, lover, or something else. And besides," I asked him, "if the relationship is so damned significant, then why have you had seven of them over the past two years?" I'm sure you understand my confusion over these mixed messages.

So one can only try to guess what some of the real meanings of these SLIMED titles are in business. I've tried to construct some samples, so that you get a little practice in learning to read the Bullshit.

First, when the following titles were first used in the professions indicated below, they had pretty clear and universally understood meanings.

Term in English	When used in relation to	Means
Counselor	Social Services	Social Worker
Counselor	Law	Attorney
Consultant	Marketing, Accounting, Business Administration	Fee-based business advisor
Consultant	Construction	Architect
Consultant	Building Interior	Designer
Associate	Law	Junior Attorney (non-partner)
Associate	Clergy	Junior priest or minister
Engineer	Electrical/Electronics	Professionally trained technical developer or builder
Engineer	Shipping or Railroading	Professionally trained operator of heavy equipment
Representative	Public Relations	Spokesperson
Representative	Business	Authorized Agent
Representative	Politics	Elected official, delegate legate, or envoy

Over time, however, some meanings for these same words, standing alone have been adopted into SLIME by those not in the traditionally recognized professions.
Ostensibly the purpose is to glorify these jobs by making them sound like something they are not.

Here the operative mode becomes, once again, learning to read the Bullshit. Once these titles have been SLIMED, they are considerably more difficult to understand, which, of course, is the purpose.

SLIMED Title	English Translation: Typical meaning when term is used alone
Associate	Salesperson
Representative	Salesperson
Customer Representative	Salesperson
Technical Representative	Salesperson
Solution Engineer	Salesperson
Field Representative	Salesperson
Territory Manager	Salesperson
Application Engineer	Salesperson
Consultant	Salesperson
Counselor	Salesperson

And progressing from there, it becomes even more complex as these terms are used in SLIME in conjunction with modifiers. It's becoming even harder to read the Bullshit.

SLIMED Title	When used with	in English Means
Application Engineer	Software	Computer Programmer
Application Engineer	Decorating	Housepainter
Application Engineer	Daycare	Changes Diapers
Field Representative	Insurance	Claims Adjuster
Field Representative	Electronics	Computer Repairman
Field Representative	Landscaping	Sod Roller
Consultant	Furniture	Furniture Salesperson
Consultant	Personal Transportation	Car Salesperson
Consultant	Sanitation	Janitor

It is my understanding that those who construct much of the new terminology in SLIME reside in Hiring/Firing, departments. This is where SLIME was first used to rename that very department itself, first as Employment, then Personnel, and now Human Resources, while still retaining its original function of hiring and firing.

The first documented use of SLIME actually occurred about thirty-five years ago, when a clerk, Merwyn Lemmelstein, decided to adopt the functional title "Human Resources Staffing." It sounded really neat. Later, even though there wasn't anything involving technology, Lemmelstein decided to throw in the term "Technician." I am told by those who are in a position to know, that Lemmelstein thus became the first "Human Resources Staffing Technician" on record in North America.

My guess is, that since Lemmelstein didn't want anyone to feel bad about what they did for a living, it was considered a good idea to employ a little Bullshit to preclude this from happening. SLIME, in it's early days as a language, provided the perfect medium for this to happen.

And, at a minimum, since almost everybody wanted to make their own job sound like something more than what it was, the trend was born.

Translations

Next we come to descriptors that totally destroy any possible connection between SLIME and the English language. These terms have changed so radically from their original meanings, that one simply cannot guess at their true meanings. Therefore these SLIME terms can only be translated in order to be understood.

Here are some examples of how SLIME has been used as an outgrowth of the "Political Correctness" movement, (which is neither political, nor correct, but has come into widespread acceptance as a means of avoiding lawsuits.)

SLIME Term	English translation
Physically Challenged	handicapped
Financially Challenged	poor
Vertically Challenged	short
Educationally Challenged	ignorant
Intellectually Challenged	stupid
Morally Challenged	dishonest
Mortally Challenged	dead

Taking this one step further, here's how some of these SLIME terms might typically be used on the written portion of an exit narrative for an employee not surviving his first ninety-days' probationary period:

"We were inclined to work with Mr. Grivahnitch to expand his job knowledge equity. Upon further investigation, however, we became aware of his being educationally and intellectually challenged by the position. In addition, working as a monetary collections and disbursements technician, seemed to provide a continued quandary to his morally disadvantaged predisposition."

Consider, as an alternative, how my Uncle Jack would have handled this same situation in his grocery store in the fifties. It would have sounded something like this:

"He seemed nice enough when we hired him and we would have worked with him. But money kept disappearing out of the cash register. Then we caught him red-handed. We learned too late. We were stupid. The schmuck lied to us. Not only hadn't he finished high school, he had served time for theft."

But the problem doesn't end there. Since SLIME is a "softer" sounding language and much more pleasing to the ear, large organizations are adopting it as the standard means of communication when trying to find nice words when they do something really shitty to their employees or customers. I'm sure you know some of these already.

Statement in SLIME	English translation
With available programming services	You pay extra for this option
Pre-owned	Used
Specially selected for our Fall Sale	We found the cheapest off-shore produced shirts we could for this sale to maximize our profits
We'd like to pursue "vendoring out" your job functions.	You're gone, we're hiring freelance.
We'd like you to consider becoming part of our "contracted" contributors.	You just lost your benefits and are now paying your own social security and self-employment tax.
Our goods are commensurate with costing factors.	Our stuff is crap, but it's cheap.
We'd like you to play a part in our current efforts at "downsizing."	By becoming part of it. Adios!
We feel that you need to have the opportunity to balance your inventory in order to help your organization benefit from full-line selling	You'll take the Prius too, or you don't get any Camry's.

Based upon the above, one could make a case for the term "Territory Manager" in SLIME being defined as someone who "manages" to stay in his job as a salesperson for more than six months. His boss, on the other hand, who would have been called a sales manager in English, would probably be called a manager manager.

Nevertheless, this doesn't simplify the mess we've gotten into. One might hypothesize that the solution is to chuck everything and start over. There is also a growing segment that supports another view. They say that if we are going to euphemize everything by converting it into SLIME, can't we at least try for a little more honesty. This is a paradox of the first order and herein lies the key to SLIME.

They have missed the point entirely. The purpose of SLIME is to avoid honesty.

Exercise:

After having mastered the basics of SLIME, see if you can determine what the following statement means (taken from a product description in a Fortune 500 company.)

"(Product Name) was considered to be on at least a par with the top five `normed' products included in the category selected for evaluation. (Product's Name)'s specific functionality performance in this regard, again, consistently ranked in a singular class of achievement that was truly not replicated by others measured in aggregate, or individually."

Now, practice doing this yourself, substituting SLIME, for English. See, it works. SLIME makes almost any crap sound better than it actually is.

Rose's Rule of Business #9: Find new meanings for old words to hide the true meaning of what you have said when the truth doesn't serve you well.

Standards of language are now so loose as to allow for custom and usage to dictate new and contradictory meanings for old words. Therefore, as you rise to the top, it is perfectly acceptable to include a few of your own in the new lexicon. In this manner, you can weasel-word anything you do, or have done, to sound like an accomplishment.

XIII. Seasons of an Employee's Career:

Just like our society in general, most big company cultures are built on lying. This usually starts out in the job interview. The terms "Marketing, Creative, Manager/Management" while having well-documented meanings in English, can take on other one's when the people using them are speaking in SLIME. Here's a situation I found myself in back in the early days of my career.

When Your Sales Are Down, Misdirect All Job Applicants Into Sales Positions

My creative director's job at one agency wasn't all I had hoped for, and I was thinking of making a change. At that time, creative directors were clearly in the concept, design and production end of the business, while account executives were almost universally in sales. Job postings typically reflected this.

So naturally, when I went on a job interview for a position that had advertised "Wanted, Creative Director, Technical or Engineering Background" I thought that was the position I was applying for. So imagine my surprise, as the interview with the agency president, took this path:

I was ushered in, introduced myself, put my portfolio down and listened as he began to talk.

"Very few people really do a good job of presenting capabilities to a potential customer." he began while looking at me quizzically.

"True enough." I answered to let him know I was interested in what he was saying, while I wondered what he might be leading up to.

"In fact, it takes a special kind of person to find the right mix of capabilities, schmaltz, and creativity to secure a commitment."

I wasn't getting his point. It sounded like double-talk to me. I'd been expecting him to ask me about my creative philosophy, projects I'd worked on, the types of technology accounts, and so forth. But I nodded anyway and listened. He continued on about the creative process, how agencies interfaced with customers, and what should be a good "fit" between agency and customer.

I waited patiently and finally got a chance to get a word in. "I'd like to hear a little about the creative director's position you have open." I asked.

He looked at me amusedly again, as if there was some subtlety I had yet to grasp, and started all over. When he stopped, he had not even come close to addressing my questions.

After all this swerving and dodging, I was beginning to get pissed off. So I pressed him for a direct answer. "Could you just answer one question? Are you or are you not looking for a Creative Director, like your ad says?"

He answered with great intensity, as if his energy could substitute for directness. "The person in this position will be …just…a total nut… for customer contact, and will be responsible for securing contracts for the agency."

I'd been SLIMED.

"Are you talking about a sales job?" I asked, my patience at an end. If so, I had just wasted about two hours.

He still did not answer me directly. Instead of a simple "yes" or "no," he continued on. "The exceptional individual who is accepted for this position, will have the rare opportunity of both creating solutions to business situations, and of selecting those clients with which to work."

Suddenly it was clear. This guy was looking for someone to not only reinvent the wheel for each project, but to cold call or prospect, and in his terms, "secure contracts" for the agency. It was not only a sales job, it was a snow job.

At the end of the interview, he passed me off to the head of account group management, who introduced himself as "the sales guy." His name was Hutchings "Hutch" Fenwick. He was tall, blond, muscular, talked in sports metaphors, had light blue eyes, a cleft chin and a neck somewhat wider than his head. In other words, the perfect person to represent an agency as the head of sales in New Corporate America. I got the feeling I'd met him before.

Hutch began telling me all about the agency's commission structure. After seven minutes of him talking without taking a breath, I knew my only out was to interrupt. Madeline tells me it's rude, and she herself will listen to someone for hours before uttering a peep, but I'm not that polite.

"Excuse me." I said. "You must have mistaken me for someone else. I just popped in looking for directions to the men's room. Could you tell me where it is?"

"Oh, yeah." he said, sheepishly. "It's like… down the hall, and like… to the left."

I waited for five minutes in the lavatory, then peaked out the door to make sure nobody saw me and sneaked out.

In that interview I had learned some new techniques:

- When you are really looking for salespeople, write the ad in SLIME.
- Avoid direct answers or eye contact.
- Be as evasiveness as is necessary to suck in the applicant.
- Pass the prospect off to someone else to answer questions you should have answered.
- If the prospect is still listening after the first two hours, you can probably intimidate him into taking almost any shitty job.

The people I've referred to, were doing what they should have, but were not sophisticated enough to suck me into a creative directors job and then switch duties on me.

Seasons of AN EMPLOYEE'S job in Corporate America
   Spring

For this person, the air is fresh and full of promise. Each morning brings a brilliant dawn and he (we use "he" generically to mean he/she) can't wait to get to work. This is also the time when we can suck him in and get him indoctrinated.

At this time, both entities need each other. He needs a job, and we need him because he has a skill set and just enough experience help our business grow.

He's grateful for having the opportunity to contribute. We milk this for as long as we can until he smartens up.

We have an air of expectation, and give him clues about what that might be without ever truly stating them.

- So he throws his heart and soul into it.
- He comes early.
- He stays late.
- He takes work home with him.
- He learns all there is to learn about the company.
- He learns about the market.
- Once he begins to understand, he makes plans for how he will contribute.
- He communicates that to his superiors.
- Naturally, we take credit for his ideas when we pass them on to our superiors. (Even a CEO has a board of directors, even if that just consists of a wife.)

- We are temporarily pleased and begin making plans based upon his work.
- During this time, he has several successes that indicate to us, that he really does know what he is doing.
- He believes that he is beginning to forge a comfort level with us.
- This initial period usually takes about one to two years for most situations.
- When his credentials are firmly established within our organization, he is ready to move on to the next season.
- He has plowed the field, and begins to plant it.

Summer
- Things are beginning to heat up and there's work to be done.
- He has now identified what it is he can contribute.
- He has given some examples of it.
- He prepares to roll his programs out on a large scale, and we support him in doing it.
- Here's where he begins to get some notoriety for what he is doing.
- Others in the company besides are now aware of his early successes.
- At this point all others begin to take their fair share of the credit.
- They want "in" on what he can do for them.
- So the cheerleaders get behind him.

- Others commit money and people to his projects.
- Some become jealous and try to horn in on his success.
- It is a time of great excitement and also of great risk.
- But since he has done this once or twice before in his career, he knows that he will be successful at it.
- He has planted the field and begins to water it.
- This can take another one to three years, typically while he waits for germination, and plans for harvest.
- Meanwhile, we continually lay application upon application of manure on this person.

Autumn
- It's been a good growing season.
- His knowledge and contribution to the company have now matured and he has been successful.
- He can document a very profitable harvest.
- We take the wheat and give him the chaff.
- Using his success, he has taught his skills and knowledge to others.
- The others who will continue to get better at taking credit for his work try to unseat him.
- Nevertheless, he has groomed them to assist him in what he does to increase the contribution to the company.

- Not only that, he has found new areas in which his experience will increase the contribution to the company.
- He is now ready to go into another phase.

Winter
- He is now neither plowing, planting nor harvesting, but has determined how to expand planting for the next cycle that will yield an additional cash crop.
- He identifies still further goals for both himself and the company as well as plans for achieving them.
- His experience has taught him that this is where the greatest payback comes from.
- This is where we can start to take his accomplishments for granted.
- We can harvest the fields he has planted for years without your presence.
- So what the Hell do we need him for now? Nothing. Getting rid of him is where the finesse comes in.
- We now take all credit and tell him that he sounds like a rooster that crows at sunrise thinking he has made it happen.
- We now have others who have well documented his success and believe that they can do what he has done as well and at a lot lower cost to us.

Keep in mind, everybody you cut is money in your pocket.

- In addition, most of the disciples he has trained are much younger and make less money. This too, means more money in your pocket.
- Now, as if by magic, his status changes.
- You now call him into meetings and tell him things like "The company is taking on a new direction. We must tighten things down a bit. We have to determine which of our staffing functions are `must haves' or only `nice to haves'"
- We can then start excluding him from key meetings, isolating him in effect.
- We can reclassify his job and tell him he is now working on "special projects" but give him nothing to do. He'll leave soon enough.
- If he doesn't leave, you can then fire him for not producing those "special projects."
- We can then repeat the process with others at a lower cost of overhead, and can always hire another bunch of worker bees at still less money. We can always pitch them in the creek too, and hire another bunch. And remember that's more money in your pocket.

This ends the rotation of his seasons.

Now here's a thought for you: Ever see those columns in the business section of the newspaper titled "Promoted, On-the-move, Business Leaders," etc.? How about the newspapers doing a section right next to it called "Canned?"

I've often thought that someone could have a lot of fun with that. Can you imagine some of the subsections:

- Fired with Prejudice
- Fired without Prejudice
- Downsized
- Outsourced
- Failed to Progress
- Failed to Grow with the Needs of the Company
- No Longer Fit with Company's Strategic Goals
- Squeezed out in Hostile Takeover
- Squeezed out in Friendly Takeover
- Now Excess to Company's Needs
- Skills Replaced with Lower Cost Options

The above were taken from **The HR Director's Handbook of Accepted Phraseology**, Chapter 11, "*How to Blame the Blameless When You Want to Cut Your Payroll.*"

But I digress.

My experience and that of many of my colleagues tell me that the "Seasons" can take from as little as three years, to a maximum of about seven. This is typically how long it takes to get big business development programs going to the point where they will continue to produce for a number of years in a "maintenance" mode. Big companies know this also. But in order to distract your subjects, so that they don't catch wise to the fact that you know this we can play a lot of little games. That's where the company culture part of it comes in. We'll discuss that in the next chapter.

Exercise
Here are some common mistakes people make as they go through the seasons of their careers in an organization. You need to perpetuate these mistakes in order to maximize what you can squeeze out of them before they catch on:

- They believe a supervisor, peer, or subordinate is a friend.
- They train an associate to do their job.
- They make their job look easy and someone else tries to horn in on it.
- They actually make their job easy for a subordinate to do, in order to delegate.
- They excel at something that doesn't require it
- They get their job done too efficiently.

Rose's Rule of Business #10: Get rid of any employee that has passed through the seasons of their job.

As senior management, your job is to cycle these underlings through their seasons as rapidly as possible. You may even think of it as an assembly line. Remember, if they slow it down even a little, that's money out of your pocket to keep them on the payroll.

XIV. Corporate Culture - The Religion of Business

As I promised in an earlier chapter, this is the Private Sector version of what I had experienced in the Air Force. There are some important nuances that make this somewhat different. You'll easily be able to see this difference.

Whereas government organizations are more homogeneous with regard to Culture, every CEO seems to have his own that applies to his company. This is typically fueled by our particular delusions of grandeur. I don't care who it is, we all have it, or we wouldn't have scratched and clawed to get to where we are. We want to be recognized for something, and we will stop at no expense to get our employees, customers and fellow CEO's to pay us this respect. The important point here, is that this delusion of grandeur sets the whole tone of the company's culture.

When Andy Warhol said that everybody would get their fifteen minutes of fame, they all believed it. You know what I'm talking about:

During the 80's it started with a guy who bought a small personal electrical appliance company. On national TV, he stated that he was so impressed with this product that he "bought the company." Well, I was impressed with him because he had that much money.

You know this next guy, too. You've seen his clothing commercials. He states "Our suits do not cost quite as much as you would expect to pay at a department store." Then he adds, "You'll like the way you look. I guarantee it."

What is it that us CEO's all have in common? We are, after all, big wheels because we have money and can go on national television. People should be impressed by us. This in essence, is a type of marketing in and of itself, Marketing By Ego. I've learned that our products sell because we are larger-than-life people. Why wouldn't the little people want to buy our products and have some of our glamour rub off on them.

Malcolm Baldridge and the Search for the Holy Grail

This pervasive sense of ourselves translates into each of our companies having their own culture. The culture is nothing more than a vehicle through which the CEO will accomplish his goals and get his notoriety. The individual who works for him has to hold steadfast to the key espoused or stated principle. Anything less is treason.

More importantly, all marketing activities play to this one principle. the bosses ego. But bigger companies have more money.

The Malcolm Baldridge Award was still something new when I worked at B.S. Inc. thirty years ago. Companies like Cadillac competed for it (and eventually won it.) You remember my affectionate references to Axel Hoel, (The Big A.H.) a few chapters ago. He would have liked to have thought of himself in the same class.

I know what you're thinking. "Yeah, sure, a multi-million dollar schlock agency competing with a multi-billion dollar manufacturer of quality automobiles. Like it was a real contest."

So one day, The Big A.H. straightened his bad rug, (Babs made him wear it.) and called one of his famous all-company meetings in the warehouse.

He smiled his expansive smile as his VP's passed out candy bars while we filed in. With him on the dais, an improvised platform of wooden freight pallets, was Zoella Zinzniz, B.S. Inc.'s training manager, (and official cheerleader). She had a smile on her face too, but it masked a very fearful look. I'd gotten to know her, and realized that this was her "I've got something very exciting to tell you" face, when in fact, she did not. It was this one quality that endeared her to the Big A.H.

"I've got something very exciting to tell you." she said, predictably, and pensively, as if about to be garroted "that I'm very excited about." she repeated.

The Big A.H. looked at her sideways, and she smiled broadly.

"We're going to have an exciting Quality Program at B.S. Inc." Zoella said, as if telling her husband that they were expecting a child, "and we're all going to participate in this exciting program."

This meant more candy bars. I like candy bars.

Zoella outlined the program and then The Big A.H. gave us a few words. He told us it would take Service, Sacrifice and above all, Commitment. It might take us years to achieve his goal, but that he would pursue it no matter how long it took. This was impressive stuff.

Now, quality, in the theoretical sense is okay. I mean, I have nothing personal against it. And up until that point, I thought we produced a pretty good grade of schlock. Despite all the internal goings on, the creative team was one of the best in the country.

Let me give you a for instance:

At that time, one of my recent projects was for a company trying to sell farmers manure tank treatment pellets to neutralize the smell of the contents. Honest! The company had settled on a tri-fold, four-color visual, and a videotape that would get their point across. My first offering had been a before and after scratch and sniff panel. No shit! I thought we were on a roll. And we'd made a lot of money on that one.

So I didn't understand what the point was. Did this new announcement mean that our schlock wasn't quality schlock?

What became clear in the next several weeks, was that this was part of the new wave of Corporate Religion that was to sweep the Fortune 500 for the next fifteen years. The Big A.H. had seen a way to capitalize on it in two ways; his ego, and profits.

I'll explain. The first part of it, catered to The Big A.H.'s ego, because he really believed, at first, that he had a chance at the award. All we had to do was prove that our quality program generated results that meant a quality product. But more importantly, it gave us a rallying point.

In order to understand how this worked, you might liken it to ISO 9000 certification. You map out a process and then prove to the certifying authority how good you are by sticking to your own plan. This is good, because it allows you to set low expectations, and then consistently meet them.

What this meant in terms of the Malcolm Baldridge Award was that the little people had to come up with some simple problems that essentially didn't exist so that they could then "solve" them.

It was patterned after the indoctrination used by the Communist Party. The process of doing it went like this:

First, those who granted the award needed to see that the supplicant company had "seen the light."

We needed then to apologize for being wrong to begin with.

Next, we had to appear as if we were making a great commitment and sacrifice as we put in place new quality-engineering processes that would miraculously solve the problems we had invented.

At the same time, we needed to show that as a company, we'd had an epiphany and document it for other proselytes to read.

It was Bullshit of the first order, really high class stuff and it made me feel proud to be part of it. The momentum was so great, that everyone either got caught up in it, or got fired.

So, you may ask, how did we incorporate this into our own marketing program?

It was relatively easy. We spent the next six months in teams, taking seminars from professional seminar givers. After that, we began by creating solutions that would solve problems we could then invent. Next, we invented the problems to which we already had the solutions and then went about the process of solving them. Then, whenever we had our little get-togethers in the warehouse, The Big A.H. would start out by asking who had anything to report. And right on cue, someone would stand up and said in a loud voice, "I'll testify...I'll testify!"

The Big A.H.'s ego was truly infectious. We found ourselves going around the four-building complex saying things like. "Gee, I'm really excited about our Quality program."

or...

"I'll bet that B.M. (our business competitors, Business Motivators,) doesn't have our quality program."

After a while, we got creative. One day in a staff meeting, I found myself saying "I can foresee a time when others will emulate our Quality program." I was practicing for the day when I, too, would be a CEO and have my own Company Culture.

Keep in mind however, that my immediate goal was to continue getting a paycheck.

In fact, I was applauded. I was quoted in the company newsletter. This was my fifteen seconds of fame. I even framed the newsletter and took it home with me. Madeline hung it in our downstairs bathroom directly across from the toilet so that friends could see it when they visited.

But I Digress

Then I had my turn to testify. It
reminded me of "Show and Lie" when I was in
grade school. But here, we were actually
encouraged to tell bald-face lies, if not by
direction, by inference. It was really fun and
great practice for my eventual CEO-dom.
I demonstrated to the rest of the group
that by using the new word processors that
were catching on, we could easily duplicate the
Bullshit we produced for one client and modify
it for another, as long as they weren't in the
same industry. It was easy. All we had to do
was change a word here, a phrase there. It
allowed us to essentially double-bill for the
same material, and do it with fewer people.
Remember, this was money in Axel's pocket,
and I hoped that I'd get at least a little part of it.
Of course, we had been doing it that
way all along, but The Big A.H. didn't realize it.
I just made it sound like something new. Word
processors just speeded up the process. The
people it freed up could be used for other,
more creative pursuits.

B.S. Inc. had other plans, however. This was the second way in which B.S. Inc. was to capitalize on the program and was really indicative of a more sinister agenda to be followed. What quality really meant to The Big A.H. was scrap and rework, cutting costs, tightening the belt yet another notch and exploiting his people to the point where he could get another 5 hours a week productivity out of them, while using the output of the teams as eyewash to submit to the committee for the Malcolm Baldridge Award. The net result was that when we got done with the quality program, we were temporarily able to produce as much Bullshit with 722 people as we had with 815 people. This meant another $5.5 million in Axel's pocket.

Of course, most of us who are CEO's, can't spend much time on any one task or program, and couldn't stay on task for more than six months without a new program, or reorganizing, or both. So after submitting for the Malcolm Baldridge Award and being told that it was only open to manufacturing companies, he got pissed off, junked the Quality Program and went on to the "Community Spirit" program.

I was disappointed and felt bad for the Big A.H. He had tried, and I was having fun with the program. My group and I had gotten really good at manufacturing problems.

But the real benefit of our "corporate culture" program, was that we had prototyped a new trend that we had taken to our customers. We started an entire new division that marketed such "quality programs" to other corporations. The big A.H. made millions from marketing this high-class Bullshit, until Corporate America caught wise and starting producing their own.

I am proud to know that I was at the beginning of this movement.

But again, I digress.

Since B.S. Inc., I have seen or employed this phenomenon at every major company I have worked for. Usually there's some cheerleader who is the CEO's instrument for announcing the program, as if he or she was one of "us."

There's an almost universal script they go through while presenting this. Here's how it goes. You can fill in the blanks with one of the "buzz" words that follow:

"I'd like to tell you about our new _____ program at Mega-Putz Corporation. A recent Wall Street Journal article said that _____ is the wave of the future. Companies, large and small will be measured on their _____ programs. At Mega-Putz, we are committed to the principle of _____. We will be asking each and every one of you to make a personal commitment to _____ in your area of expertise. In the next week or so we will be forming _____ teams, and you will be assigned to one of them. We will spend the next three months learning the principles of _____, and then the next three months applying them to _____ target areas in our own organization. Then for the next six months, we will measure our _____ program and document our progress. We are confident that at the end of one year, the complexion of Mega-Putz will have changed significantly due to this _____ program, so that it will be an entirely different and excitingly new company.

- Quality
- Benchmarking
- Just-in-time Manufacturing
- Re-engineering
- Wellness
- Throughput
- Forecasting
- Interconnectivity

Just for kicks, substitute the term "*ignorance*" for one of the above.

I'd mentioned earlier about how "getting the money first" was relevant later in my career. Here's how: I hired on to be Director of the Communications Group. The original deal they offered was that If I developed $1 million in communications business within one year, I would get a bonus of $20,000, but they wanted to hire me for less money to start off with. We both knew I could develop the business, so they tried to sell me on the benefit of having a really big bonus at the end of the year. Of course, the catch was I had to be in that particular job, at the end of the one-year period. I had to admire their cunning.

I, on the other hand, knew from their reputation that they'd figure out some way to screw me. So I said that I'd take half of the $20,000 as part of my base salary. This would be a good and fair salary for my services. I told them I would be content to wait the rest of the year to get the other $10,000. (I knew I'd never see it.) Reluctantly, they went along with it.

Once I got my program rolling, things went better, and quicker than even I had anticipated. I dove into it with ferocity. I traveled all over the country, wherever there was an opportunity. I developed the million within the first six months, with another million plus for the second half.

My overzealousness was a big mistake, however. Objectives met, they re-shuffled the organization and put me into client programs as a program director thereby eliminating my original job before the end of the period. No cigar. These guys were good and I decided I'd use this tactic myself when I had the chance.

In the second position as a program director, my job was writing incentive programs. Here, I was also promised financial rewards. I was to receive 1% of the total merchandise, travel or other incentives purchased by my clients. Of course, by eliminating this second job in another "restructuring," six months short of the redeeming cycle and moving me to another department, they got to keep the one per-cent. But with the higher starting salary to begin with, I'd been making good money right along.

I knew I'd never get the huge bonuses. No one at B.S. Inc. ever did, save one or two V.P.'s, and of course, The Big A.H.

Ironically enough, he had forgotten about the Malcolm Baldridge Award, while a succession of V.P.s had passed this mandate on from one to the next. Relentlessly, they kept applying, until nearly twenty years later, after the award committee had greatly broadened the categories for participation, B.S. Inc. actually won the award.

Exercise

Try to determine what aspects of Corporate Culture apply to marketing your company's products or services and how they apply to the life of the little people. Refer back to Chapter X and review the list of questions regarding how far you would go to protect your own survival. Then ask yourself if the little people truly pay allegiance to your Company's Culture. For example, do they know the following:

- Where the prayer meetings are held, Warehouse, Cafeteria, Auditorium, Off-site hotel or retreat?
- To what god do they pray, i.e. Quality, ISO 9002, Malcolm Baldridge, Benchmarking?
- Who are the lay-leaders in the congregation? Do they inspire others to be like them?
- Do they subscribe to the canons of your church, i.e., mapping, flow-charting, prosaic documentation?
- What is the liturgy? Do they know it well? If asked by outsiders, could they defend it?
- If God grants them children, will they raise them in this church, (i.e. provide a second-generation of employees?)

Rose's Rule of Business #11: Convert to the new Religion. You can always convert back.

Accepting religious conversion (sometimes known as "corporate culture") is a must. When joining your company, this is necessary for the little people to become part of the faithful. You may then guarantee their longevity for as long as is convenient for you.

XV. OLD WORDS, UPDATED MEANINGS:

If we are to believe the popular business press, corporations still adhere to the "old" principles. This is confusing, since corporations say one thing and do something else.

Let me give you an example. In one of the companies I worked for in the last twenty years, the new CEO decided to take an employee survey. Among the questions answered about the "quality of life" in the corporation was one concerned with the concept of job security. Most employees understood and agreed with the idea that there are no guarantees, and that if the company is not doing well, then all jobs are at risk. What the real issue here however was the capricious downsizing, outsourcing, or contracting of jobs, when the company was doing well.

So the CEO, held employee meetings in all the divisions to let the employees know that this mood was going to change, and that he was going to do something about it. He didn't want his employees constantly worrying about their jobs from day to day.

The corporation bought corn poppers for all the divisions and sold popcorn from 11:30-12:30 every Wednesday in lunchrooms throughout the company. The CEO therefore designated Wednesdays as "popcorn day." Corporate also bought two newspapers on Fridays and placed them in the lunchrooms of each of the divisions and allowed the employees to wear casual attire. Fridays therefore became known as "casual day."

The CEO continued to issue updates regarding the new culture that he was creating, drove home the message of continuity, corporate family, truth, and moral rectitude.

Then, just before Thanksgiving, he announced a reorganization that eliminated two-hundred people including thirty-five senior managers, directors and VP's.

This came on the heels of four quarters of record earnings. On top of that, the stock dropped, after announcing this. I have a friend who is a stock broker. When this happened, he told me, "The market hates good news." As a counterpoint to this, when a popular stock dropped because the company's earnings dropped, he told me "The market hates bad news."

My conclusion is that the market hates any news.

During that same period of time, I was writing a story for a local business paper, and was invited to a chapter meeting of Assholes Anonymous. The membership consisted of wife beaters, tailgaters, an axe-murderer, marketing people, a number of child-molesters and three Twin Cities area CEO's.

The dynamics of the group was interesting, as the rest of the group totally shunned the CEO's. I was able to ascertain that the issue was one of credibility. During these meetings, penitents share their pain with each other. This is the only area I know of where and honesty by CEO's is not only desirable, but expected. The CEO's were incapable of this. Regrettably, even Assholes Anonymous had minimum standards and therefore excluded them from further membership.

The point here is that without an understanding of the type of bald-faced lying and evil expected by a CEO, you are doomed to failure the New Corporate America if you want to become one of us. Understanding it will arm you and put you in the right frame of mind in order to succeed.

With the help of some of my friends, I've identified eight of the principles that are constantly invoked by CEO's, as if they mean something, when in reality, there is no substance to back them up. Again, there might be more, but this is a start. The concepts are:

- Loyalty
- Fairness
- Ethics
- Quality
- Value
- Honesty
- Decency
- Responsibility

I'll deal with each of these concepts one at a time.

Rose's Rule of Business #12: If you cannot find examples of these concepts as part of your company's values, manufacture some examples. Remember, Joseph Goebbels said "Invent the Big Lie. The Bigger the Better. People will believe it."

Although the terms "loyalty, fairness, ethics, quality, value, honesty, decency, and responsibility" in conjunction with "Business" seem mutually exclusive, business, continues to use them. This is because meanings change over time. Therefore, this use makes them subject to the broadest of all possible interpretations. As a CEO, you should dictate the custom and usage of these terms to your greatest possible advantage.

XVI. Loyalty

Loyalty is a great concept that can help you get more productivity out of your workforce. But what do you do with your product development people when you want to milk what you have for a few years and cut overhead? You need to insist on loyalty from your employees. This can take many forms. Typical expectations include spending long hours at work, foregoing a personal life at times for the "good of the company," and staying in lock-step with the company's party line. And for this, of course, we promise our loyalty in return. Promises explicit or implied include continued employment, and delivery of the benefits that have been promised, such as pension or retirement plans. But you should never have to deliver on those promises, or take any of the blame for not doing it. After all, you are providing employment and benefits for as long as it is convenient for you to do so.

Suppose you want to just milk your product line for a few years and not have to put anything back into it. This is a two-pronged strategy. First, you cut off your product development funds and tell your product managers that they will just have to be creative. This money drops to the bottom line and becomes a source you can draw upon for your compensation. Of course, without a nickel to do even do some basic research, they become powerless.

Then, when they have no new products to show in development, you can sack them for non-performance. This saves a big chunk of change. Remember, if you don't do it, ultimately it comes out of your pocket.

This also makes the bottom line pretty for your stockholders or Board, and becomes the basis for your bonus. This is where your loyalties should lie.

You're only as good as your last game

I had been with the Disgusting Bodily Substance Removal Instrument Division of Meg-Orifice for about four years when our double digit growth dropped to single digits. Compared to the rest of the economy, however, we were pretty healthy.

After two consecutive quarters of only eight and nine percent gains, our product development leader, Floyd Rasmussen, a twenty-year company veteran, got the sack. Floyd was an engineer who had worked his way up the ladder the hard way, and had contributed greatly to the growth of the company for many years. He was two years away from full retirement at sixty-five

I will admit that I was a little surprised that our CEO had done this, but after a while I realized that our parent company, Meg-Allied Neurological, U.S. (Meg-ANUS) had done this in all of their subsidiary companies. It was a master stroke and improved our stock price by double-digits, which meant our CEO's position was secured for a long enough period to collect all of his accrued bonus options.

Floyd was eventually replaced by Troy White, a new CEO (no relation) when product development had to start up again a few years later and direct management of the function fell under the CEO's duties. Mr. White had some good qualifications. He was blond, good-looking, and told good golf stories. He was at least fifteen years younger than Floyd. He reminded me vaguely of someone else I had met over the years. He had served as Vice President of Competitive Sabotage in his prior job at another Meg-ANUS division.

Mr. White began holding a series of "open" meetings, in that his staff selected cross-sections of employees throughout the company. The meetings were mandatory. He smiled and told us we were on the verge of a quantum leap in growth. By now, it was obvious to most of us that what he said didn't ring true, but it was hard catching him outright.

I remember asking a buddy at one of the meetings "How do you know when he's lying?"

"Whenever he's in the room." was the reply.

Finally, Mr. White swore that Meg-ANUS would stand behind the division and ride it out. He pledged that his "door was open" to any and all who might want to see him.

As US product manager for the Abradatron, I was in a position to help. I had identified hospital groups around the country who wanted their own private-labeled product. We had more than enough capacity, and it would have added millions to our volume. Floyd had been against it, however. He'd doggedly held to the position that we needed to increase our own branded lines before taking this route.

But the rest of the management team was all for it. With Floyd gone now, all I needed was Mr. White's approval. I found that Mr. White's open-door policy only extended to having meetings with his direct reports, which included his vice presidents, his administrative assistant, his bookie and his driver. At the time, I was only at director level. Despite my calls and the one-page executive summaries of my ideas, he ignored me. I wondered why.

After two weeks of trying unsuccessfully to see him (although his office was within 100 feet of mine,) all advertising and promotion budgets were pulled. Development had already been done on two of my new products already and I couldn't see how stopping the rollout would be logical. I came to the following conclusions:

- The open meetings had merely been window dressing for him to buy time to plan his budget cuts.
- Meg-Orifice was seeking to develop new markets and new products but wouldn't let me pull the trigger.
- Meg-ANUS was not going to stand behind us little people.

- Top management was either going to spin off the division, or put it into a "cash cow" position.
- In short, Mr. White had blatantly lied to us.

I was in trouble. If there was to be no new business revenues, my job was toast.

Man Up When The Going Gets Tough...

I talked to my boss, Ralph. He agreed that perhaps what Mr. White said and what he did were in conflict with each other, but that Mr. White had a plan that he was not at liberty to share with others, at "this point in time." Ralph told me to be patient and to trust that there was a purpose to what was happening. He said that the more important job now would probably be restructuring the organization. Now more than ever, he told me, my loyalty to the organization was important. It would take all of us working very hard to get back on track. I had already lost two quarters of my new business plan to the stoppage of funds and my contribution to profit was way short.

I drew my usual analogy about people being the locomotive that pulls the train and that disconnecting them from the cars behind would mean that the train would eventually stop and that in order to get it going again, it would have to be the people who provided the motive force.

Ralph knew this and indicated that at some time, Mr. White would have to recognize this truth, but that for a period of time, any new business development programs would have to be placed on the back burner, but the staffing would still remain to pull the "train" in another direction.

He also promised me that when the restructuring came, I would have a place in the new organization, even if it wasn't in business development, but that I would still be there to resume those duties when they were deemed necessary. Besides, they "had a lot invested in me" according to him and couldn't afford to let me go. Then he suggested that I begin working on some new programs anyway. When Mr. White realized that this function would need to get going again, we would be ready.

The shit-heel alarm in my head had already gone off. Something was up. This was the equivalent of a six alarm fire. It was time to get busy, but not with new business development or marketing programs.

Part of our company culture was that it was real easy around Meg-Orifice to be a slacker. One might say that this was our corporate culture. No one ever checked up on people. This, of course, was due to the fact that most people were scrupulously conscientious and there was no need. Reluctantly, however, I came to realize that it was normal operating procedure for people in high positions to simply sign out for days at a time as "working out of the office," "meetings in other buildings," and so forth. In fact, this practice was quite pervasive.

So I figured "What the heck, why not give it a try." I clearly had been thinking too small.

I stopped my idiotic practice of coming in at seven and leaving at five-thirty.

I began signing out, "doing research, working out of office," etc.

I spent my time at the library researching local companies that might use my talents.

I updated my resume.

I updated my network.

I spent more time working out.

I stayed home some days and watched videos.

I began recycling my old projects, as new work, with "search and replace" on my computer. This is what I would show Ralph when he asked me what I was working on. (In the years since my time at B.S. Inc., I'd gotten real good at this.)

About two months into my new schedule, I found I was a lot more relaxed. I wondered why I hadn't done it before. I had discovered a whole new way of working.

But I digress.

About that time, it was announced that there would, indeed, be a restructuring. We were not to worry, because this would not be a reduction, just a reallocation of resources.

I had a revelation in my dreams that night. In my dream, I had gotten to work the next morning and all the office cubes were empty. On the wall, painted in three-foot high letters were the words "You're all fired!"

The following day, I was asked to structure a new position that would upgrade the duties of the job I'd had previous to being U.S. Product Manager. This job had been running our Office of Practice Development. It would be a director-level position. Still, I was concerned. Again, I asked Ralph. He was part of the restructuring task force. He reassured me.

"Ay, buddy, you're part of the team." Ralph said. "You've busted your hump. You won't get hosed. Besides, no one else schmoozes with the sales force, or our customers like you do and we need your computer expertise." According to him, I would be rewarded for all my hard work.

"Schmuck," I muttered to myself.

Just in case, I quietly began preparing the first volley of letters and resumes to fire off when "Execution-Day" arrived.

The mood around the office didn't change. It was like a ghost town now. Everybody was signed out for "meetings at other buildings" or "working out of the office."

Going Up The Packing House Ramp

Meanwhile, back at the boardroom, Mr. White scheduled a company picnic at noon on the Monday prior to Thursday's scheduled restructuring announcement. They put up a tent on the grounds, hired a banquet catering company and even had band playing. It reminded me of the Titanic.

I watched as he walked among us non-entities and told us "not to worry." He reminded me of a couple of guys I knew in the Air Force who did black ops. He had the eyes of a stone killer. He told us there might be some discomfort, as a number of us would be reporting to different directors or VP's but that it would all work out.

"Asshole," my shitheel alarm repeated over and over again.

I got to the office at eight on Thursday. The phone rang at eight-thirty, and I was summoned to one of the conference rooms.

I went confidently. When I got there, along with my boss, Ralph, was our H.R. manager, P.J. La Croix. My spirits momentarily brightened. Perhaps P.J. was there to go over my new grade level, new higher salary, and increased executive perquisites with me.

Ralph motioned and I sat down.

When Ralph began, speaking to me, I knew I was in deep shit. The language he used didn't even sound like him.

"I regret to inform you that due to the current restructuring, your job is no longer viable in the new organization. We appreciate your efforts in helping structure a new position that will enhance the new organization, but have selected another candidate to better balance the management structure of the company."

I'd been SLIMED.

Not only had I been slimed, but by somebody I'd almost come close to partially believing, (well...sort of.) In English, what he said, meant, "We're screwing you. We'll fill the job you so naively structured for us, with some minority at less money. Now please have the good grace to leave quietly."

My mind went into shock and I must have gasped audibly before I could leave quietly. Ralph reacted to it for a second but then picked up the beat again.

"We have grief counselors in the room next door to help you deal with the situation. And you can take the rest of the day off, if you'd like. I'm sure you'll want to call Madeline. You can clean out your office tomorrow, which will be your last day with Meg-Orifice."

That was it. There was no fanfare. They let go several hundred people including thirty-some managers. I'd been sold down the river.

They gave the new job to a woman with little experience for it. They paid her about half what they had paid me. It gave the impression, however, that they were trying to create gender equality. But they screwed her, too. She was not able to do an adequate job and quit due to frustration within three months. This, I am sure, was part of their plan. Almost universally, they had placed a second tier of people in positions where they couldn't possibly succeed. This meant that most would quit of their own volition and that the company wouldn't have to offer them a package. I felt bad for my successor when I heard about it. It reminded me of what Mega-Flake had done to Rochelle Marks.

So the organization had filled a quota, and at the same time, had planted the seeds to eliminate yet one more person. This type of sabotaging is common. Putting a person in a position beyond their qualifications is only one way. Isolating them from their peer group or assigning them to a new and unreasonable reporting official are but two more. There are dozens.

The bright spot in all this, however, was that at the tender age of fifty, I was beginning to get a little smarter than I had been at forty.

On the day I received my one-day notice, the job search volley I had prepared included fifty-three targeted letters and resumes ready to mail. Within a short period of time, I received offers from three of those companies and took the best one of them.

I learned an important lesson. Lying plays an important part in the concept of loyalty. What I had learned, was that it doesn't pay to be loyal to, or care about people who don't care back. But it is important to give that impression. Loyalty is a one-way street. It is quite possible for an employee to feel something in the way of loyalty towards their superiors in a company, but the reverse is seldom true.

One final note. In my last interview with my soon-to-be ex boss, I asked him. "What was all that crap the last few months about loyalty being rewarded and staying the course?"

He just laughed a sheepish, embarrassed laugh and said. "I did what I could."

"Right." I replied flatly.

"By the way," Ralph asked. "Could you get me copies of those new marketing programs you've been working on, just in case we need them?"

"Sure. I've got hard copies for you and disks." I said of the old projects I'd recycled. I knew that Ralph and his boss would never catch on, perhaps even try using some of them.

Just as a point of reference, one of my "insider" contacts at Meg-ANUS headquarters told me that Floyd had been axed because corporate had determined that he had integrity.

"There's no place for integrity in business." my contact told me.

These actions were all good lessons for me in becoming a CEO. Clearly, I had been thinking like one of the little people. I needed to start thinking like Ralph did and our CEO, Mr. White (I repeat, no relation.) Regrettably, I had started to develop a modicum of integrity, but it wasn't too late. I could nip it in the bud.

Exercise
In order to better prepare for your job as a CEO, ask yourself the following:

- Can you develop new ways to give the little people the impression that you are loyal to them while developing new ways to rid yourself of them when they are no longer valuable to you?
- What core activities are really necessary for you to give this impression to the little people?
- Can your HR staff determine how many actual hours it takes the little people to do their actual jobs while still milking the cash cow?
- Can you delegate some of this to your cadre?
- Can you get these same people to develop their best work for you when you are about to fire them?
- Finally, when you've run out of new products or services, can you give your Board the impression you are moving projects forward without actually doing so?

Rose's Rule of Business #13 Loyalty is a one-way street, and it accrues to the company.

Loyalty to employees ruins otherwise great business programs. The reason is that once employees actually believe you are loyal to them, it only ensures an endless supply of mediocre work. Therefore, you need to give the impression of loyalty to them, but still engender some degree of doubt.

XVII. Fairness

Business tries to give the impression of at least attempting to be fair. To wit: Political Correctness. Some even inadvertently achieve a little fairness. After all, to quote an earlier chapter, if you play at it long enough, it isn't play anymore.

But human nature being what it is, pragmatism should always supplant any attempt at fairness, given the chance.

We've all experienced this fairness in business to one degree or another, or have known someone who has.

I wasn't mature enough yet, to ascend to the CEO-dom of a major organization and was still learning from some of the masters. The following exemplifies how one CEO survived it and what I learned from him.

In the 80's, I worked for the engineering division of Mega-Score, a schizophrenic educational test-scoring company. The engineering division was but one of seventeen personalities the company presented to the purchasing public. This included public school districts, universities, psychological testing facilities and the government. These separate personalities were vestiges of companies that were at one time either acquisitions, or completely autonomous departments that were started in the 60's and left to their own devices.

It became apparent to me when I hired on, that the company had absolutely no centralized marketing function whatsoever. Moreover, people in positions of power in the seventeen divisions, either ignored each other, treated each other with enmity, or at best, regarded each other as competitors. And the relatively new company CEO, Alberto "Mad Dog" Gelati supported this position.

I must explain that Mad Dog got his nickname quite innocently.

There was a famous comic of the 60's and 70's who made his living doing an impression of someone with Tourette's Syndrome. At that time which pre-dated political correctness by at least two decades, Tourette's Syndrome was thought to be humorous. Being of a certain age, and a certain look, Bert Gelati reminded people of this famous comic. When they would comment on it, Bert never thought this was anything but a nuisance.

But that all changed one day, as Bert was skateboarding around the lake on his estate. He hit a bad bump, went sailing off the skateboard, and hit his head on the pavement. This strange quirk of fate, the resulting head injury, actually gave Bert Tourette's Syndrome.

Initially he tried to hide it. He avoided his next round of quarterly speeches to stockholders and employees alike. Typically, these speeches bored his audiences and put them to sleep, which was just fine with Bert. It kept them from asking any meaningful questions. Then one day, shortly after the injury, Bert found himself in a situation where he had to address the employees.

He decided to tough it out. During a practice run, he tried just biting his tongue if he felt anything inappropriate coming out. And except for one extraneous huff, and one or two "son-of-a-bitches," this worked just fine. The "son-of-a-bitches," and an occasional "huff" his PR expert told him, would be simply interpreted as giving his speech emphasis.

So when he got in front of the crowd, he felt he was prepared. But as anyone who has spoken before an audience knows, a dry run is not the same as the real thing.

Bert began speaking and felt something inappropriate bubbling up. He bit his tongue to block it. Instead, what came out was a growl. There were a few titters in the audience. Bert continued undaunted, but the next time, biting his tongue wasn't quite as effective. Out came a "YIP!" There were a few more titters, but the audience quickly settled down. The third time Bert tried biting his now sore tongue, out came the full-fledged bark of a German Shepherd.

This time, the employee group broke out in hysterics. But instead of being embarrassed, Bert found he enjoyed this type of attention. It was an epiphany to him. No longer able to keep biting his pained tongue, he decided not to hold back, and see what happened. He finished his speech laced with "asshole's and motherfuckers" thrown in and the audience laughed uproariously. They loved it. Instantly, someone coined the affectionate term "Mad Dog" for their CEO and it caught on.

The following month he tried it with the stockholders, and they too were entertained.

Another revelation to Mad Dog was that rather than being a detriment, he found the Tourette's syndrome to be an advantage. It kept people slightly off balance. This was especially true given the climate of Political Correctness and the values of a society that had switched from being achievement-based to esteem-based. Besides, his audiences didn't know what was coming next, so they paid attention.

After a year or so of speeches to shareholders, investors and employees, he had fined-tuned the non-gratuitous parts of his performance around his affliction, and decided that his act was ready to go on the road. He tried out for one of the local comedy cabarets and was pleasantly surprised when they granted him a permanent weekend spot.

But I digress.

Mad Dog was fine with things the way they were with Mega-Score having no centralized marketing functions. In fact, he repeatedly told us that this was healthy. Each individual division would grow its own revenues, and employees could guarantee their own welfare by contributing in this environment. He also promised that while we were a cash rich company, our very structure would make us unattractive as a target for takeover by a larger company.

My division president repeated this message. My mandate was to develop programs for our division only and ignore the others. I took him at face value, and began my programs.

But after our first successful marketing program I began hearing from my colleagues at three other divisions. I was told that I had a lot of nerve communicating with their customers. They told me I was to stop it immediately. Then I began receiving hang-ups and anonymous calls that stopped just short of death threats. I was not only stunned, I was angry. I'd seen corporate paranoia before, but never on such a widespread basis.

Then one day, Kyle Smith, one of my more sanguine counterparts in one of the other divisions across town stopped in to see me. We'd had lunch a couple of times, but had never gotten past pleasantries and sports talk.

"I like your programs." he said in a straightforward manner.

It took me by surprise. "Is this a trap?" I asked.

"No, seriously, Jonah." he continued. "You've seen some of mine. We have the same mindset. I think we should work together."

"Now I know you're putting me on." I responded. "Besides, if they catch us collaborating, we could get shot." It was rumored that the last two guys who had tried it disappeared and were never heard from again.

But he was serious. During his eleven years at Mega-Score, he had taken it into his head that instead of having seventeen different sales organizations and seventeen marketing organizations, we might be able to ride on each other's backs, since many of us called on the same people.

What he laid out made sense. We would have to, of course, get the okay of our respective division presidents, but that wouldn't be a problem. We invented the term "piggyback" for our programs, indicating that they belonged to only one of the divisions, and that the other was simply riding along. This neatly avoided the appearance of any centralized marketing function. The only problem, was that we had to develop these programs as "off the books," or as black ops, so that Mad Dog didn't get wind of it.

Individually and jointly, Kyle and I continued to lobby Mad Dog to create a centralized marketing function by showing him the benefits of doing so, only to get thrown out of his office repeatedly.

At one point, Kyle got nervous. "You know, Jonah. If we keep this up, they could fire us. What'll we do if that happens?" he asked me one day.

"Screw `em." I said. "I was looking for a job when I found this one. I'll find another. So will you." I meant it. I'd always felt I'd rather be shot for a goat as a sheep. Somehow, I'd figure out how to meet my living expenses. I always had. In the meantime, I wasn't going to be influenced.

Over the next year, the two of us began some very successful marketing programs, in that they got noticed. I don't believe we actually sold anything for the company, but at least customers began calling and telling us "Hey, we didn't know you did that too," or "Geez, we didn't realize you were the same company."

Then, as the decade came to an end, someone asked if we had a website. I'd been in and around the computer and network business for thirty years, but I was still a skeptic on this account. I believe my initial response was "I think the internet will be the pet rock of the 90's."

Kyle, being the good buddy he had become, told me that I was full of shit and that I had one of the great marketing minds of the nineteenth century.

So I went home and mulled this over. I decided he was right on both counts.

I spent more time surfing the net, such as it was at that time and actually started looking at other businesses. From this early start, we decided to contact our IT people to see if we could get some space on our mainframe to start our own website.

Once we were up and running, it didn't take long for the other divisions to see the value of this. They all wanted in. Thus was born our first Corporate Internet Governance Board.

This time, Kyle and I went to great pains to get legitimized and got Legal and MIS involved as our sponsors. Consequently, the Internet Governance Board got on Mad Dog's radar screen. We were even given a budget. But subtle things began happening.

During his first two years with the company, Mad Dog had taken under his wing, several empty suits. One of them was a salesman from our printing division who sold blank scoring sheets to schools. His name was Dick "Hutch" Hutchford. He was tall, blond, muscular, talked in sports metaphors, had light blue eyes, a cleft chin and a neck somewhat wider than his head. He looked familiar to me. I introduced myself, and we became good friends. I had the feeling that he was going places in Mad Dog's organization. He began coming to our monthly meetings as Mad Dog's personal representative. He would invariably take a seat next to me, place his laptop on the table in front of him, but never opened it up or turned it on. He would watch, seemingly in awe, as I made notes during our meetings on my laptop, and asked me after each meeting if he could get a copy of my notes.

"Sure." I would respond. "I'll e-mail them to you."

"Jonah," he would ask, "could ya like print `em out and send `em to me, like in interoffice mail?"

Gladly, I complied.

After about six months into his tenure, Hutch made another request, "Hey Jonah, do you think someone can show me how to turn this thing on?" he whispered, pointing to his laptop computer.

"Sure." I said, and then undertook to teach him basic computer operations, and finally applications. In about three weeks, he was able to turn it on, open his e-mail and read it, but he couldn't reply.

The following month, Mad Dog announced that he'd made a change to his Leadership Committee and had appointed Hutch the chairman of the Internet Governance Board.

After that, the prime movers of the IGB, which included me, Kyle and Sheila Wildung, (a former Maryknoll Nun and teacher-turned MBA) from our Florida Division, proposed that we divide the group into several subdivisions. Whenever we met, we started currying favor with Hutch by buying him happy meals to get him on our side. It worked. One of the subdivisions was Marketing. Hutch rubberstamped it for us and we were on our way. Now that Hutch was our (nominal) leader, Mad Dog started coming to our meetings himself, and even encouraged our activities.

Kyle and I, and one other marketing director at this point, began putting together our first company-wide marketing program. We got real buy-in from other divisions, in that they allocated funds from their budgets for these projects. Mad Dog was aware of this, but still held fast to his vision of having "no centralized marketing."

In the meantime, we were growing. In the years I had been with the company, we had grown from 300 to over 400 million in revenues. Marketing and internet activities were only partly responsible, but they were getting us noticed in places we'd never done business before.

Next, we grew from 400 to 650 million in revenues.

During that time, Mad Dog decided that marketing was the more important function of our group, and renamed our committee the Mega-Score Corporate Marketing Committee.

But other subtle changes began happening. In a corporate reorganization, another empty suit that Mad Dog had placed under his wing, Bradley White (no relation) was promoted from sales clerk to Marketing Director of the Scanner Division. He replaced my buddy Kyle. Admittedly, Brad had some good qualifications. He was blond, good-looking, and told good golf stories. He was at least fifteen years younger than Kyle. Kyle, in the meantime, was moved out of his office into a cube and told to write a new business development plan for the scoring market in Yemen.

In yet another reorganization, the Engineering Division was combined with and placed subordinate to the Scanner Division. With this, change, came a personal one for me. One Thursday morning, I tried to access my on-line forum as one of the executive members of the Marketing Committee, and was locked out. I quickly called MIS and told them of my plight and they told me that I had been taken off of access.

I spent most of a day trying to determine who had made this mistake. I got nowhere. I tried again on Friday, and found that none of my fellow Committee members were available to me. Then, at 4:45 that afternoon, my boss, our division president, called me into his office and told me that Bradley White was now our executive member on the Marketing Committee. End of issue, but not of story.

I spent a miserable weekend thinking about this, and then came to work on Monday to the news that Mega-Score had been sold.

"Sold?" I asked one of my colleagues.

"Sold." was the answer. "To Mega-Book."

"Who the Hell is Mega-Book?" I queried.

"Damned if I know." my colleague answered.

Turns out that Mega-Book, a Mega-Billion Dollar British company, owned most of the educational book publishers in the World, and wanted us not for our engineering or our scanners, but our school management software and our knowledge of how to get content such as books on-line, so that they could electronically sell it to schools.

So in the six years my marketing buddies and I were working our plan, Mad Dog had done the following:

- Positioned the company for a takeover despite his protestations to the contrary
- Placed his two empty suits in key positions.
- Packed his golden parachute by purchasing $14 million in company stock just prior to the buy-out with a loan from the company that was "forgiven" by the board after the purchase.

The stock doubled in price afterward.

About a week later, it was announced that since there were two division presidents within the Scanner Division, only one was necessary. Consequently, my boss was given the axe. In retrospect, I should have realized from his demeanor when he told me about my being replaced, that he already knew his own job was at risk, if, in fact, he hadn't already been told.

During the multiple speeches Mad Dog gave at the various divisions, he kept insisting that the whole spectre of the buyout had occurred within a matter of days, weeks at most, and that it had been in the best interest of the company. Never mind that we had been approaching a billion dollars in revenues, were cash rich, and really had few competitors in the U.S.

Later, we learned that months' worth of due diligence had been going on. Despite this, the 850 million in revenues Mad Dog had reported, had included over 265 million in booking revenues that never happened.

Within weeks of the buy-out, our division and several others were disbanded, and hundreds, including me, got their notices. This included any number of people who had fallen into the "company line" to help ensure their jobs. It hadn't helped them a penny's worth. And Mega-Book found this additional downsizing necessary to reduce spending, and generate quick cash to come up with $50 million in the short-term just to service the debt on their $2 billion purchase price.

One final note: With his golden parachute assured, Mad Dog announced his retirement, and Mega-Book announced his replacement, Don Numnutz. Don was the president of the Testing Division that had screwed up high school competency testing for a Midwestern state just prior to the buyout. The company was being sued, and Don was responsible. Fuck up and go up. It also turned out, we learned later that Don had worked for the President of Mega-Book's U.S. operation prior to coming to Mega-Score.

So what does this all mean with regard to fairness in business?: When you are in charge, get your people to do an extraordinary job so that you can reap the benefits and get a fair shake for yourself.

Despite my exuberance at Mega-Score, I never really got emotionally invested to the point that I couldn't extricate myself. During the six years I worked there, my friends would periodically ask me how things were going. My reply was almost always. "They pay me so I show up."

I also knew going into this job that I have the look and the persona of a "sidekick" or a playmaker. I'm short, gray-haired and chubby. In order to get top jobs in Corporate America, you need to either be tall, and if not Nordic-looking, at least handsome or pretty. If not that, then you have to be extremely devious and good at screwing other people. I am proud to say that I had developed my talents to fall into the latter category and get a fair shake for myself.

Ironically enough, when they disbanded my division, Brad White took over all marketing programs, but didn't have anybody left to do them. So his division president called me in and asked if I could stay on for awhile and help Brad. I went to Brad and asked him what he was looking for, and it became evident that he was looking for a short analysis and plan for one of our internet-based businesses and a direct marketing program for scanners. This was about a week's worth of work for me, and something I could easily clone from some of my previous programs.

"What type of format are you looking for?" I asked Brad.

"I dunno?" he replied. Clearly he didn't. Upon further questioning, I determined that he had never seen a business or marketing plan, let alone write one.

"Give me some options." he said.

I returned the following week and told him that what he wanted would take about three months. I was sure that would give me enough time to find another job and not use up my severance package. It did. Six months later, Brad's division president was gone too, and Brad was placed on Don Numnutz' staff.

Interestingly enough, after the stock market decline the last couple of years, Mad Dog's stock declined precipitously. But his weekend job was going well. I heard a got an engagement performing and opening act, or warm-up as they call it, in Vegas as an oil Sheik with Tourette's who gets lost in Crown Heights, Brooklyn. Story is, he really packs them in these days.

Exercise:

As a CEO, ask yourself the following questions.

- Are you now capable of double-dealing with your executive committee while still retaining their trust?
- Can you package your company for a successful takeover and keep it under wraps long enough to double, triple or perhaps quadruple your compensation and golden parachute?
- Can you then make it seem as if the sellout just happened to fall into your lap?
- Can you perhaps indicate that you had no choice? This can be done by feigning health problems that preclude you from continuing to work on behalf of the little people.
- At the end of this can you feign great regret and even shed some tears at a farewell speech to gain sympathy?

Rose's Rule of Business #14: Above all else, to thine own self be fair.

As a CEO, you must find a way to achieve some fairness for yourself. This is the true meaning of "fair" at your level.

XVIII. Ethics

My experience tells me that ethics in business are relative rather than absolute as we were taught in Sunday School. Ethics in business are tied to a perverse kind of morality that is defined by what top management thinks. Here's how it works:

Invent The Big Lie And Stick To It

Mega-Cleft espoused a high code of ethics. It was stated in our literature. Our salesmen verbalized it to our customers. Our engineers were forced to memorize it. What it said was this:

"We will not manufacture or distribute a product unless it meets the highest standards of quality and has been proven in clinical trials to be an effective treatment."

This may sound a little naive to you, but I think that it might have actually been true at one time. If so, it certainly pre-dated my involvement with the company.

By the time I had taken over as VP of Product Management in Mega-Cleft's industrial-strength surgical nose-hair excision division, we had gotten caught up in a technology war with our competitors,

They had introduced a product that rhinologists didn't have to adjust anymore. We therefore, had to come out with a product that was not only self-adjusting, but self-cleaning. This required us to get the product on the market in a shorter period of time than the typical five-year clinical trial cycle.

Make a Commitment to "Grey" Areas

This meant that Mega-Cleft would do what all other companies do in such situations; give ourselves permission to cheat. Since Mega-Cleft always had several clinical trials going at one time, with products of somewhat indeterminate characteristics, they could always find doctors to back their theories, given enough money. Although they were aware of it at the time, we were not aware of any FDA efforts to stop this practice.

Most doctors are decent enough. There even exists some documentation that suggests, upon occasion, a doctor or two has actually cared about the people they are treating. But there are always some who are willing to go along with questionable practices in order to benefit personally.

But I digress.

Legitimate clinical trials are set up with very strict protocols. Physicians and surgeons who conduct them are paid to conduct them according to these protocols and very carefully log a series of case studies. Again, most of them do exactly this.

There is a "gray" side to this, however. In addition to paying the doctors to do the clinical studies, some companies will also pay them, for example, an additional $500 or $1000 per patient to do a "marketing study" on the patient, i.e., an exit interview. Some say this is a just a way of window-dressing bribes. On the other hand, without these incentives, clinical trials would never get completed, and then, who does that benefit? Nobody.

So let's theorize that Dr. Smith makes it known that he can be influenced, and has a choice between using Mega-Cleft's Rhino-Jet, or the Debo-Nase, made by our competitor. For using the Rhino-Jet he gets paid an extra $500 by the manufacturer to do a "marketing study," while the product is in clinical trials, plus his normal surgical fee and any other stipend he is paid for doing research. For using the Debo-Nase, he gets only his surgical fee (unless they, too, are in clinical trials.)

Suppose further, that after the clinical trials indicate that the Rhino-Jet is reliable enough to go onto the market, the manufacturer will continue to pay him $500 each for extending the marketing studies.

Consequently, it is in the best interest of the doctor to help get the product that provides him with the most income on the market. This leads to packing in as many case studies in a clinical trial during a given period of time as possible. It also opens the door to backdating some of these cases to shorten the time to market. Consequently, it pre-disposes these doctors to use this product and not give the patient a choice in terms of which one to use.

Now let's give Mega-Cleft and these doctors the benefit of the doubt and look at their side of it. We will assume that these doctors knew instinctively that our product was better, and were helping to prove what they already knew.

In Mega-Cleft's estimation, these doctors were just being creative in establishing an alternative to a longer clinical trial. "Packing" of many patients into this short time frame, whether or not the patients asked for the treatment, was done with the best of intentions. The French, Italian and German medical communities do it all the time. And after all, isn't time relative, anyway?

Many doctors also take the paternalistic attitude that all patients are ignorant of medical treatments. Therefore, they need someone who knows more than they do to be an advocate for them, or in fact, select the appropriate treatment. It could be further stated, that if these ignorant patients had known the treatment was available, each and every one of them would have opted for it anyway. Mega-Cleft management was sure of that. In effect, then, if you follow this perverse logic, Mega-Cleft was quite altruistic in its fostering of these types of clinical trials.

Mega-Cleft sold more product, and of course, the conniving doctors made more money from the marketing studies.

Price Increases Substantiate Added Value Due To Perception

Such was the case with the Rhino-Jet 2, "The Next Generation." This was an absolutely great product from the company's point of view. It was priced a thousand dollars more per unit than the previous product. (We were paying $500 each for the "marketing studies" and had to recoup it somewhere.)

This additional cost just got charged to the patient's medical coverage. It was considered, therefore, by both the company and the doctors to be a non-issue.

The Rhino-Jet 2, "The Next Generation" was also cheaper for us to produce. And it had features that our competition didn't have.

Therefore, the perception due to the increase in price, automatically gave it added value.

There was only one very small, almost insignificant problem with it; some of them were just a wee bit defective.

The previous product manager had known this and failed to pass it on to me. That was easy, since the defect really didn't show up until it had been on the market for a year. Two weeks prior to that time, he abruptly resigned and left the country in the middle of the night to accept a position selling rental car returns in the Argentine (where there is no extradition treaty with the U.S.) It was a great career opportunity for him, we were told. That's when I was moved into the position.

When I learned of the problem, a cover-up was already in progress. I didn't understand why, and began writing a plan for a recall. I was told to stop work on it. In fact, I had been given the job of writing a position paper indicating that any "anomalies" experienced were as a result of improper sizing on the part of the doctor. Most of these surgeons had an average of twelve to fifteen years of experience in surgery. As you could have guessed, the company felt that they would readily accept this criticism from marketing people who had absolutely no medical training.

Upon further research, I found the following:

Damage or injury to patients could be limited since nine-tenths of all of these units were still on shelves in hospitals.

Only about twelve percent of the units were affected.

We could effect a recall immediately and replace the Rhino-Jet 2 with the previous model, with which we had experienced no problems.

We could correct within about thirty days, the defect in the Rhino-Jet 2 by reworking the twelve percent of returns that were defective. Those that weren't defective, could be re-sterilized, re-packaged and sent back out immediately.

Even though a recall would be costly, about $1.1 million in actual dollars, I thought it was a good plan. Thinking this was my first and most critical mistake. Along with the recall, in order to appease top management, I had developed a recovery plan for recouping the $1.1 million. I could get the re-work done and turn the whole thing around in three or four weeks.

"No," I was told by our VP of marketing and sales. In a twisted type of logic, he said "It wouldn't be ethical. We'll just work through it."

"Ethical?" I queried. "Isn't the bigger question about being straight with them?" This was my second big mistake. I was beginning to redevelop a sense of absolute as opposed to relative, or situational ethics, which, as I've said, has no place in business.

"Then what about the ethics of letting our stockholders down." Came the reply. "If news of this ever gets out, our stock will drop." I felt shamed by my inattentiveness to this point. He was right. "We'll just go out to the field with new technical literature telling how to properly size the Rhino-Jet 2, to avoid the problem." he continued. "We'll make a running change in manufacturing to correct the problem. Eventually, the hospitals will work through their shelf stock. It's already been decided. We'd like you to work with Dr. Charleton. He's agreed to write an article for Partners in Probosces."

This referred to the surgical newsletter Mega-Cleft published that went out to rhinologists all over the country. And "Chainsaw" Charleton as he was referred to by his fellow surgeons had barely kept his license due to his poor skills and questionable practices. Nevertheless, he often acted as the "beard" for our company and some of our competitors to legitimize some of our questionable practices.

Please don't think for a moment, that my bout with absolute ethics had resurfaced. The mere hint of my having absolute ethics could have caused me to lose my then good standing in the American Business Community.

But supposing I were caught at being part of a cover up? Going to jail would have been hard on my family. I had visions of seeing myself on 60 Minutes, microphone stuck in my face. "Mr. White, what did you know, and when did you know it?"

So I did the only thing I could. I purposely sabotaged the position paper I'd been told to write by finding all the internal roadblocks to getting it done. That was easy. After two months I still had not come up with much more than an outline. That was when our company president ended my involvement with the Rhino-Jet 2.

I was promptly replaced, and "kicked upstairs," to another department, far away from product management.

The next product manager had no compunctions about the project. He'd come from the aluminum siding and windows industry. He completed the position paper and went on a road show to demonstrate how to get around the defect in the product. Naturally, he was well received by "Chainsaw" and was introduced to quite a few of Dr. Charleton's colleagues.

Manufacturing never corrected the problem. Eventually, surgeons simply migrated to other products. By then, we had all abandoned this particular sinking ship.

From the foregoing, I have developed the following theorem: Zidel, in his 1988 study noted a similar inverse relationship between liability and personal accountability, but that's a subject for another book.

As the prospect of liability rises, the tendency to adhere to an absolute code of ethics declines.

This can be expressed graphically in the following table:

Rose's Law of Relative Ethics

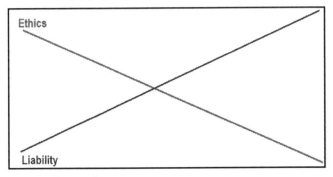

Exercise

Try the following to determine what the relative ethics are in any situation:

- What is your franchise with your customers, i.e., do you have credibility with them?
- In case of a total screw-up on the part of your company, is there a possibility that they will believe what you tell them?
- If you lie to them, will you be found out?
- If you are found out, can you cover with more lies making it sound like miscommunication?
- Can you get away without saying anything and just indicate that nothing is wrong with your product in the case of complaints? During the 90's when a major U.S. auto manufacturer was receiving well-

documented complaints that its minivan rear-deck latches were faulty, they conducted a massive recall without ever acknowledging they had a problem. They were just doing it for "good will."

- Can you get away with saying that the customer is not using the product properly?
- Can you get away with saying that the customer's sloppiness causes the product not to work? Don't think this is peculiar to American Business. When numerous problems were documented with seatbelt retractors from cars of Japanese origin, a spokesperson addressed the American press. He indicated that since Americans are such sloppy eaters the problem was due to food that had dropped into the retractors, and that the same cars in Japan had no such problem.

If you can answer any of the above in the affirmative, you are an effective CEO and your company is a good candidate for using Rose's Table of Relative Ethics. It is also important to note that there must be a high **Weasel Factor Quotient** within the company to make this work. (Refer back to Chapter VI.)

Rose's Rule of Business #15: Ethics is the title of a college course, nothing else.

It is a good thing to hold to a higher standard of ethics as long as it is convenient. When it is not, ethics become relative. Therefore, in marketing any product or service, one must subscribe to a "flexible" code of ethics in order to get the job done.

XIX. Quality

Q: Do you know who benefits from all of the quality programs undertaken in the U.S.?

A: The consultants who teach the classes.

The reality is that many companies market crap. Regardless, they try to convince their customers and themselves that the products and services they market are high quality.

Let's take a typical scenario.

You already know of the high regard in which I hold "The Big A.H." from Business Synergistics, Inc.. I'd like to tell you more about the quality program we had when I was working there. I've held this part back because it directly affects our discussion of Quality as a concept.

As I'd mentioned, it all really started when "The Big A.H." was reading Fortune or Barron's. He either got fearful that his customers hadn't heard the word "quality" liberally sprinkled in the printed Bullshit, or video Bullshit that his Bullshit writers were turning out.

So he immediately called his staff together and formed a task team. "We need a quality program" he said.

"What... have we been producing schlock all this time?" one of his minions replied ingenuously.

"Certainly." The Big A.H. replied. "That's what we do. But we still need to let our customers know we're a quality schlock house." he said.

So he hired a consulting firm that he'd read about. They had developed a process for improving the perception of quality in large corporations. It was at that point, that we'd had an all-company meeting in the warehouse to introduce the program and mandate that everybody at B.S. Inc. had to learn the process and put it in place.

During the three months we were learning the process, a leadership team comprised of The Big A.H.'s vice presidents was at work on a parallel track to identify goals. His cadre worked hard at it during this time of corporate renewal. They held three, four-day meetings; one in Palm Springs, one in Acapulco, and one in San Francisco to accomplish their part of the job. They said that they needed to get away from the offices to "get a fresh perspective." (I would have suggested the Abbey at St. John's just outside rural Collegeville, MN, for their off-site meetings.)

When they were done, they had produced a half-sheet of paper, on which the goals were written. They were quite satisfied with themselves, as they should have been for all their hard work.

- Error Reduction
- Productivity
- Scrap and Rework

At that time, "The Big A.H." sponsored a contest to name the quality program. One of the guys who worked in the warehouse, Harry Hamhander spoke up. He'd been around a long time. "Hey, I gotta idea. Back in the sixties, when I was in the service, we had this lieutenant, can't remember his name. We had this quality program, and he starts doin' things like makin' up problems and writin' bogus reports to the brass about how we solved 'em. They bought it. We could do the same thing. No one will know the difference."

The Big A.H. nodded. It was a good idea.

Then one of the deacons asked what the program had been called.

"As I recollect, the Air Force called it Zip Defects, No Defects, Zero Defects...some baloney like that." Hamhander answered.

So Harry got the assignment of forming an official naming team. His team spent six weeks formalizing what they'd already heard in the warehouse. Consequently they officially passed on the part about "Zero Defects" to his manager who passed it on to Zoella Zinzniz, who passed it on to "The Big A.H.".

So one day, "The Big A.H." called another warehouse meeting and indicated that the executive committee had developed a new and original name for the program. It was to be called, officially, "Zero Defects."

For the next year, all people did at B.S. Inc., was go through the motions. Nothing really changed, but for two things:

At the end of the period, due to forced labor, productivity had gone up and our labor force had gone down.

All of our new literature now had a gold foil stamp or a printed seal on it that said "Zero Defects."

And in the meantime, in order to further cut costs, a few more of our catalogues had edges that were a little more jagged. We also used a little less ink, so the coverage wasn't as dense. We used a cheaper paper. We turned things out quicker, further reducing quality by increasing typos, grammar and fact errors. But we still gave it the stamp of quality.

Keep in mind it was only the perception of quality we cared about, and it worked.

The Big A.H. had accomplished his goal of creating the impression that we were a quality schlock house. That was marketable, and the point of the whole exercise.

Once, during the program, I heard that one of the printing coordinators had suggested a procedure for actually improving the cut and finish of a catalogue we were producing for a large chemical company. The only hitch was that it would cost a few cents per catalogue to do this. She also had a plan whereby we could recoup those costs on one of the other pieces we were doing for them. Naturally, she was fired.

Exercise:
Here's another simple one. Try to remember and then write down when the last time was that you heard anything sounding vaguely like this?

- "If we let the finish coat sit overnight, it will make a better product. We don't have to do anything different, just package it the next day. It won't cost us anything."

- "Why don't we leave that little tailing on the product. It will actually make it easier for the customer to use. All we need is for someone to rewrite the procedure."
- "Don't our customers ever complain about the enteric coating on the first few capsules chipping because the safety lock is too tight? We can get a better fit from our suppliers, if someone just takes responsibility for it."

Anyone who espouses such attitudes needs to be shot. (Don't do it yourself, outsource this if you want to retain "credible deniability." (More about this in the next chapter.) If you can't have them shot, at least have them incarcerated.

Rose Rule of Business #16: Don't ever improve quality in your products when pretending to do so will work just fine.

Companies do not voluntarily produce a better quality product than the minimum their customers will accept. They only give the appearance of doing so. Therefore, you may use the word "quality" as a descriptor for everything your company markets. But as a CEO you should never allow any changes that actually increase quality, lest you be penalized for it.

XX. Value

From my earliest days as a four year-old at my grandfather's knee, I remember he ran a good still and believed in giving full measure. (This was on my mother's side of the family.)

Not to get maudlin, but he used to tell me: "Some poor kid in the neighborhood is gonna plunk down a quarter that he got delivering papers for a bottle of our White Star. It's not right to cheat him out of a good buzz."

His business was made up of a lot of quarters.

Less has always been more

There were others, however, who cheated. Uncle Reuben, who worked with Grandpa and Dad would pick up a bottle of one of his competitors products and try to light a match to it. "This crap won't even burn" he'd say. Ours was at least 120 proof, and always gave a good cheap drunk for the money.

The benchmarks, of course, were the national brands. Other small companies similar to family's would typically make a custom line that included several different items to suit their clientele's tastes. But many would also shave the content. If National Brand A was a pint, some of their competition would be at fourteen or fifteen ounces. Grandpa would be at sixteen ounces. He was okay taking a smaller profit and figured he could make it up in efficiency and volume.

"These are gyp-sized bottles" he'd say in disgust as he looked at them in comparison to his. "They probably don't even use new copper when they build a still." Even at five years old, I could tell the difference.

I don't know if he got his share of quarters by giving full measure or not. I would have liked to think so, but learned later in life, that it probably didn't make a lot of difference.

Because as consumers started getting smart, companies involved in such practices as "gyp weights" started getting smarter as well in how they marketed their products. For instance, this became widespread in the cereal industry as the manufacturers began putting tiny amounts of product in huge boxes with inside packaging that was filled with air. The Ralph Naders of the World called it camouflage packaging. Eventually, legislation forced this practice to stop, but companies got cleverer still.

They began hyping what was already there and tried to make it sound like more than what it was so that they could justify charging more for it. A prime example was when the commercial dairies started using the term "creamery" with their butter. All butter comes from creameries. They really hadn't added anything to it, but used the addition of that one word as an excuse to increase their prices.

The best example, however, was when Seymour Tushman, of the National Institute for Package Downsizing was single-handedly credited with pissing off more consumers with one idea, than all of the other cheaters combined in a one year period of time.

Decades earlier, as a young man, in his capacity as Executive Secretary for the American Automobile Planned Obsolescence Commission, Seymour had already made a name for himself. By suggesting the inclusion of tail fins on cars in the fifties, and then the exclusion of the same several years later, he was single-mindedly responsible for billions in profits for the automotive manufacturers. Naturally, other industries sought his talents.

For decades, coffee had been packaged in a standard two-pound can. But in the 80's, one coffee company got a little greedier than the rest and began looking for a means of increasing their revenues.

It was at that time, that Fenwick Grelner became CEO of the Fargo Cattle and Coffee Company. He called the board together one day and asked them point blank: "How can we raise prices without anyone suspecting it?"

As was the case with most commodity products, it was subject to price changes from year to year. But in the late eighties, there was a lot of consumerism that countered this movement, when there was no reason for increases.

"I don't see how." one of the board responded. "We'd get run out of town on a rail."

"What would Tushman do?" one of them asked.

"Let's hire him and find out." Grelner said.

Tushman was brought in immediately. Two months later, the board met again.

After careful study, Tushman said, the answer was clear. He had since learned, that when a can of coffee, or for that matter, a "brick" that was packaged with flexible film was opened, the coffee would "bulk out" since it was packed so tightly. That was part of the "whoosh" one heard when opening the package or can. Therefore, he mused, how much coffee could be taken out, before anyone would notice? After all, the "whoosh" would still be there if the vacuum was still drawn as tight as it could be.

The answer in the case of the two-pound can was that five or six ounces could be removed and still cause the same sound when opened. They could still leave twenty-eight ounces to fill up the can and meet their profit goals. If adopted, this meant an immediate and automatic price increase of twelve-and-a-half percent. They paid Seymour and sent him on his way.

Once Grelner did it, the national brands were quick to catch on. The coffee producers were deliriously happy.

Initially, however, this brilliant plan backfired. People began calling the coffee producers and asking, "How come you took four ounces out of the two-pound can?"

But this turned out to be only a small hiccup. The coffee producers dissembled in their new advertising campaigns that it was now possible to get as many cups from twenty-eight ounces as was previously available from thirty-two. They spoke at great length of "mist" processing, or "natural flame drying" of the beans. The customer service phone reps were taught to be careful not to say that you could get more cups per ounce because of it. In fact, the coffee had always been processed this way. Most callers hung up within the first couple of minutes of the long scripted diatribes. But if they pressed the producers about how more cups were possible, they were told that most people didn't need to make the brew as strong as they thought they needed to in order to get nearly the same taste. Net result; make the brew weaker, use fewer ounces of coffee per pot, hence just as many cups per twenty-eight ounce can with less coffee.

Eventually most consumers stopped calling. Resigned to their fate, they continue to this day to buy the smaller cans, some of which have now dwindled to 26 ounces. There really isn't much of a choice.

Later, the ice cream companies hired Seymour. You can see his work on the 56 or 48 ounce "rounds" that are no longer half-gallons.

Cheaper Really Is Better, *For Us*

And then of course, there are the automotive companies who still rely heavily on Seymour's expertise. Due to renewed competition from American automobile manufacturers, Japanese automobile manufacturers have been feeling a real pinch for profits. Recently, one of them turned to Tushman for his expertise.

His suggestion was to eliminate the backing plate in a bumper or two. If the painted plastic fascia got bumped, it would give the cars a more "SUV" or rugged kind of look.

Learning from the coffee fiasco, Seymour better prepared the manufacturer on how to handle this. A year or so prior to introducing "decontenting," the manufacturer told the trade press that new studies in manufacturing techniques were yielding findings indicating that a multiplicity of parts is what caused automotive repairs to be so complex. The manufacturer was taking a stand and intended to do something about it.

When these changes were made, the manufacturer's spokesperson said with a straight face to the trade and general press, that it actually made the car better, because it would be easier to repair after an accident.

This was true as far as it went, since only one part would have to be replaced. But this one part was ten times as expensive as those it replaced, which also made it one heck of a lot better for the manufacturer and the repair shops. Nevertheless, they considerably cheapened the car in this fashion to make greater profits and gave the customer less in value, while attempting to say that the reverse was true. Seymour had scored a big one this time. There was a corollary precedent to this in the eighties introduced by one of Tushman's disciples, Dr. St. Germain Skulley of the Tucker Memorial Automotive Institute (TMAI). It was the collapsible, or "mini"spare. Initially, this was not considered as big a success. But, just like throwing many cow pies at the barn wall, one of them was likely to stick.

Cable News recently interviewed Seymour and asked him about his philosophy.

"The point" he said "is to find air, mist, tensile strength, elasticity coefficient or some other intangible that is already in the product but not previously identified. Then claim to have added it. Or, take something away from the product claiming to make it less complex. In this fashion," he continued, "one could make a case for eliminating the speakers from a home theatre sound system as making it less complex. Having to purchase them as "available options" would then give the purchaser "more flexibility."

Several of Tushman's customers now sell cars with half an engine. They call it a "hybrid." The jury is still out.

Seymour also gave me some other examples of words that typically get used where they have no business being:

- Cholesterol
- Texture
- Fiber

He's thinking of going to one of the American automobile manufacturers with a campaign for their cars next year that goes something like this. "The All New Avarice, Full 60 degree V-6."

Most V-6 engines have 2 banks of three cylinders each, cojoined at the crankshaft that are already at a 60 degree angle. This is a standard configuration, but most people wouldn't know this

As the need for corporate profits rises, the tendency to provide value to the customer declines.

I call this phenomenon Rose's Law of Relative Value. It can best be expressed in the following table:

Rose's Law of Relative Value

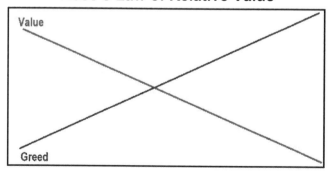

Exercise:

It's dangerous whenever mid-level management in a company starts seriously thinking about actually increasing value. When that happens, sooner or later it will get to a board of directors and look out!

Your job as CEO is to downgrade the product, make more money, and tell the customer you've actually done them a favor. Increased quality can cost more money, and that runs counter to business principles in New Corporate America.

Try to remember, and then write down if you have heard any of your company's product managers recently say any of the following. If they have, they are an infection in the corporate body and needs to be purged.

- "I don't care if it does cut into our profits a little. If we machine it finer, it'll make the product last twice as long."
- "We can get a better grade of wood for way cheaper if we just book it now. We could pass the savings along to our customers."
- "The technology to zinc coat our lawn chairs before we paint them has been around for a hundred years. If we did it, they wouldn't rust in a year."
- "Start cutting the sausage thicker. For what our customers are paying for our pizza's, they deserve it."

Rose's Rule of Business #17: If your product was any better, your wouldn't make it and if it were any worse, the customer wouldn't buy it. Leave well enough alone.

Value is inversely proportional to corporate greed. The more value given the customer, the less profit for the company. Find attributes that already exist in your products without actually adding any value. Then, find better sounding synonyms to replace these empty attributes.

XXI. Honesty

Consultants can do a lot of harm in an organization. As is the case with the others, the names have been changed to protect the innocent. (Again, they have also been changed to protect me from being sued.)

It's all in the process

When I worked for Mega-Sweat Systems, a manufacturer of recreational equipment, our company's CEO hired Killum & Baggett, a consulting group out of Boston (they all come out of Boston,) to streamline the processes we had in place for everything. Killum & Baggett's manufacturing expert, Sig Sigmund, Ph.D. had developed a process for manufacturing to increase "throughput," and decrease the manufacturing cycle time and improve quality. Naturally, they called it the Sig Sigmund Method, or just Sig Sigmund for short. A year later, in 1981, Motorola coined the term "Six Sigma" (similar sounding to Sig Sigmund) to capitalize onto Dr. Sigmund's success. The lesson I learned from our CEO is that there seems to be a symbiotic relationship between CEO's and full-of-Bullshit consulting companies. One couldn't exist without the other, but that's a story for another book.

So top management at Mega-Sweat Systems figured, "What the heck. If they can do it for Manufacturing, it oughtta work for everybody." So they authorized Killum & Baggett to set up Sig Sigmund training teams to teach this process to Administration, Sales, and Marketing.

Next, senior management assigned managers from each of these areas to form teams from their groups. For mine, this included approximately sixteen people. The drill included three days of intensive classes to learn their processes, and then weekly work sessions of four hours each.

Our task? Increase throughput for the forecasting process and decrease errors using Sig Sigmund.

Up to that point, I thought that what we needed to produce was exercise equipment. As for the forecast, we had a pretty good means for developing one already, or so I thought.

Typically, my boss Jason and I would work very closely with our market managers, sales managers, and customers to determine needs on a quarterly and yearly basis. We would do this within the context of new line introductions, extensions, promotions, etc.

We would then do what we called "roll-up" reports which were summaries from individual accounts, into regionals, divisionals, and nationals. We were generally pretty accurate, and were never off by more than 2%.

Killum & Baggett changed all of that. Suddenly, this became more than market assessments. Manufacturing, Research & Development, Accounting, Administration, and MIS to name a few, all became involved in using Sig Sigmund.

In addition, for the first time, this was set against the backdrop of getting a "Mandated Forecast Goal" set for us by our CEO, Offenbach White (no relation,) or "Off White," as we affectionately called him behind his back. There was something else new. For the first time, there was no direct contact between those of us making the forecast and the CEO. It was all to be filtered through the Sig Sigmund Forecasting Team, which was now chaired by the VP of General Administration and Accounting.

After three months of trying to adopt the process, we had our first go at the forecast. Jason and I came up with our portion, which was to be $41 Million dollars for the "Croak-Fit" line of exercise machines, "Guaranteed to get you in shape, or you'll die trying." I was Jason's marketing and sales representative. Jason was not on the team. Political researchers say that this technique, enabling people in high positions to maintain "credible deniability" first came into widespread use during the Watergate Era. Jason had used me as his foil, in order to keep himself at arm's length from this project. Perhaps they should change the term to "deniable credibility." Therefore, I carried this information into our meetings. Somehow, our forecast of $41 million got changed to $47 Million by the Forecasting Team leader, in order to meet the "mandated" goal.

"Whoa!" I said, when I first heard this uttered during one of our meetings. " Where do you get off changing our forecast?"

The answer came from the Killum & Baggett Sig Sigmund team facilitator, Moronica (or maybe it was Revonica. I forget.) Fagelbender, a short, scrawny, truly annoying woman in her mid-forties with a raspy voice. "This is what Mr. White expects." she said.

"It'll never happen. We can do forty-one, maybe forty-one, eight if we get lucky, and forty-two, three if we get sneaky. But not forty-seven." I answered. "So how are you going to reconcile what's real with what Mr. White wants?'

"Let's talk about that `off-line'." she said and blew right on past me.

Later I also asked if it wouldn't be better for Mr. White to be talking to this team directly, instead of through mediators. Again, I got the "off-line" routine. Afterwards, she wasn't available and no answers were forthcoming.

What they don't know won't hurt _us_

When I carried these tales to Jason, he was in his office, eating pistachios and throwing the shells through a miniature basketball hoop in the corner. He hadn't made too many baskets. He just smiled and told me not to worry. I apologized for the interruption and let him get back to work.

But I did worry. I continued to raise the issue at the team meetings, and finally got called into our Executive VP's office. "What the hell are you trying to do, Jonah?" he asked. "You've got to get with the program."

"This is all backwards." I said. "Sig Sigmund isn't how it's done. You should know that. You don't tell your customers how much business they're going to do with you. You ask them…nicely, and then hope they're not blowing smoke up your ass. And if we send these figures up to corporate, that's just what we'll be doing, blowing smoke up theirs. And once we do, it will kill our credibility." I said.

"Keep your mouth shut and go along." I was told. "Offy knows what he's doing. Just do your job, and nobody gets hurt."

Still, I didn't get it. How could Mr. White be so stupid as to put forth such a forecast to headquarters of our parent corporation in Dallas? Our original forecast was based upon the generally accepted marketing principle of knowing what we could sell to existing customers, give or take a few percentage points for new wins and losses.

But the forecast went forward. That and the other forecasts from the other divisions also went forward, and, quite frankly, looked very positive. Meanwhile Wall Street had picked up on this, and our stock rose sharply. Everybody was ecstatic.

Me? I am the World's worst worry wart, and knew that we'd never make forecast. Worse, I wondered if what we did had been done in the other divisions.

Towards the end of the third quarter, it became quite clear that there was to be a shortfall of several million dollars to mandated forecast. Yet, due to some pretty hard work on our part and a couple of very aggressive market steal programs I'd put together, we'd be at $44 million. This was still three million short of the $47 million we were told we would produce.

At about that time, Killum and Baggett's contract ran out, the Sig Sigmund team was disbanded and we were suddenly told to go back to doing the forecast the old way for the following year. But now, we had to come up with a documented plan that would support the current forecast.den

We couldn't figure out what the Hell was going on.

Jason seemed not to care, save for coming up with a presentable answer. He sat down with his pencil and his ever-present bag of pistachios and started playing with figures. He revised them upwards to match what Mr. White thought we needed to do and added some verbiage about projected trade-outs and so forth. Half a bag later he had his answer although both of us knew none of it would happen.

"It's still Bullshit." I said when I looked at it.

"No, creative reality." Jason said enthusiastically. "If this happens here," he showed me referring to some product upgrade trade-outs, "then this happens here." he continued, pointing to the bottom line.

"Yeah," I said, "and Osama Bin Laden is alive and well and living in Brownsville, Texas."

"C'mon, just look." he replied.

I'll admit, it was a first class flim flam. It looked good on paper, and I cheered up immediately, so Jason asked if I'd like to go out with him that night and roll drunks. It was the first time I'd felt up for it in weeks.

Jason had made a decision to overtly lie to Mr. White, because that's what Mr. White wanted to hear. Mr. White, in turn, had made an overt decision to lie to our corporate parent, for whatever his reasons.

I was starting to understand. After the final forecast went to headquarters I asked Jason how we would make up the deficit. I was afraid of what his answer might be, but he assuaged my fears immediately.

"Piece o' cake." He said. "In November, we'll start loading our distributors. We'll get them to take on extra product. We'll tell them if it doesn't sell by January, we'll let them send it back. We'll pay the shipping."

"What if they don't want to go along?" I asked.

"Some of them won't, but we'll enter booking orders anyway, and enter them as revenue."

"I'm impressed." I said. "But what the hell are we going to do in January?"

"Not my problem. I'm transferring divisions. Want to come with me?" he replied.

"Yes." I said. It sounded like a good option. I finally got it! I was reminded that when the going got tough, the tough got going. It was time for us to get going. So we transferred divisions.

What We Didn't Know Didn't Hurt Him

But what about Mr. White? Didn't that leave him holding the bag? Not really. This whole charade had been designed by Mr. White to keep corporate off his back until he could leave on January 1. He had been secretly involved for the past year in starting his own company on the side, while doing some insider stock trading to bolster his fortunes. During the time he'd been our CEO, he'd been forming a corporation, finding space, hiring people and getting investors.

Now I understood. The key here, is that honesty, like ethics is relative. Not only had Mr. White done it, so had Jason and so had I. Jason had used phrases like, "I think we should make forecast." But he never really committed to doing it. In the meantime, we had deserted the sinking ship and had saved our own hides. I was truly proud of myself for having learned some valuable lessons.

In January, when some of the distributors started to squawk, and when the booking orders got cancelled, it naturally came back to Jason through our new CEO. Jason's response, was "I was of the mindset that Fred (his replacement) had the strength to help them (the distributors) pull the product through at retail. Want me to take my old job back? I'll fix it." He knew full well that would never happen, but made the unmistakable impression that his successor wasn't half as good as he was.

And there was no real accountability anyway. Everybody could (legitimately) blame it on Mr. White. "This is the 'Denny did it' scenario."

Point being, Mr. White, our CEO (read chief embezzlement officer within this context,) the paragon with which we were to compare ourselves, the leader who had provided the example for the whole company to follow, had avoided telling the truth all around, and had ultimately jumped ship. I really wanted to be more like him.

The conclusion is that in a similar situation, this could work for you too. Just remember to use qualifiers like the following:

- It should work if…
- My initial belief is…
- We could possibly…
- We are of the mindset that…
- Conventional wisdom tells us that…
- As the prospect of accountability rises, the tendency to adhere to total honesty declines.

I call this phenomenon **Rose's Law of Subjective Honesty**. It can best be expressed in the following table:

Rose's Law of Subjective Honesty

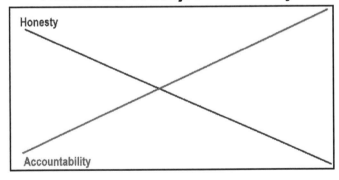

Please note that this should not be confused with the inverse relationship between corporate rank and accountability. That is a matter discussed in Chapter XXIII.

Exercise

Honesty can only be espoused in New Corporate America, if one subscribes to the concept of Subjective Honesty. This is because Subjective Honesty, when used properly, reduces Accountability. Take the above example, and play with it. Now ask yourself the following questions and grade your organization in terms of it's Subjective Honesty Quotient.

Subjective Honesty Quotient (SHQ)

In relationship to actually having to follow this forecast through the organization, which would apply? Score a maximum of twenty-five percent for each level.

_____ %	Your CEO will knowingly carry this to the Board	
_____ %	Your VP's will knowingly carry this to the CEO	
_____ %	Your Directors and Managers will knowingly carry this to their VP's*	
_____ %	Your workers will knowingly carry this to their managers*	
_____ %	Total (**Your SHQ**)	
	*Now here are two tough areas. Most workers, and many managers and directors are still grounded in the concept of honesty as an absolute. We have, however, taken this into account below. Therefore, the maximum score, realistically, is capped at 75%.	
SHQ	**Meaning**	
51-75%	Congratulations, your company ranks with the top 100 Corporations in America, since this means your company culture allows for a high degree of Subjective Honesty with your Managers and Directors.	
26-50%	No flies on you. You're still in the Fortune 500. Your Managers and Directors still aren't fully grounded in Subjective Honesty, but it's just a matter of time.	
0%-25%	Not a player, are you? Not likely that your company will be, unless you purge your VP's who are not fully indoctrinated in Subjective Honesty.	

Rose's Rule of Business #18: In Business, The result of Honesty is self-destruction

While honesty in personal relationships might sometimes be a good thing, in business, like ethics, it is highly subjective. Therefore, only be truthful so long as it is in consonance with your level of accountability. If not, bring it back in line with your relative accountability.

XXII. Decency

Here, I'd like to get one thing straight. All decency is situational. Business requires working with many other people in your organization. Therefore, it behooves the corporation to accept the myth of decency within the organization. Although most people know instinctively that this does not actually exist within Corporate America, the corporation forces them to play a role that perpetuates the myth, hence the concept of being situational.

The difference between small and large corporations, when it comes to decency is that the bigger ones are a little more sophisticated in giving the impression that they subscribe to it while the smaller ones have limited resources to do this.

Further, in order to survive in a corporation, you must dodge all manner of obstacles just to be able to continue plying your trade. It doesn't make any difference whether or not you are good in your job. Getting your job done on a day-to-day basis has nothing to do with objectives. It has to do with eliminating obstacles, namely people who stand in your way.

Applying Lessons You Have Learned

Much earlier in my career, I had watched my boss do this for years, and patiently waited for an opportunity to apply the lessons he had taught me.

I had seen him fire people just because he didn't like them and then pretend to be all broken up about it and blame it on having to anticipatorily balance the organization before HR did it. One day, in a divisional re-organization, his boss did to him what he'd been doing to others and replaced him with someone at half his salary.

Working with my new boss, Hutchinson "Hutch" Rockney gave me the opportunity to try out some of the things I had learned. Hutch was tall, blond, muscular, talked in sports metaphors, had light blue eyes, a cleft chin and a neck somewhat wider than his head. In other words, perfectly qualified to be a boss in New Corporate America. When we met, it was as if we had known each other all our lives.

Being I had experience within the division, Hutch latched onto me to "learn the ropes." He had just come from another division of Mega-Flate, where he'd been in charge of oil changes for our fleet of delivery trucks. But our division president had met him at a Christmas Party and learned that they were both hunters. He had liked Hutch, and Hutch looked good in a suit. So our division president thought, "What the heck, those guys in marketing all wear suits, so it would be a perfect fit."

Unfortunately, Hutch seemed to be having trouble with a number of the common office procedures in our division, like keeping a calendar or participating in meetings. He could attend well enough. He just couldn't participate. Writing memos, reports and using e-mail also gave him problems. He got the rest of us to do most everything for him, with the exception of expense reports, which all of us had to do ourselves. For some reason, he seemed to take a liking to me, I to him, and inexplicably, he seemed to trust me. I saw an opportunity here.

One day, after having completed his first field trip in his new position, Hutch summoned me to his office. When I got there, he shut the door.

"Hey Jonah, I'm not sure how to put this, but I, like seriously need to fill out this, uh, expense report. Could I like get some help?" he said and turned an expense report he'd been working on, sideways so that I could see it.

I immediately recognized what the problem was. I smiled. "Sure, Hutch. How can I help?"

"Well, like it's just very incredible how it don't come out. I like put the figures in the little boxes and stuff, but when I get done, ya know, it comes out minus, like I think I'm supposed to write the company a check, ya know."

"Oh, yeah, Hutch." I said trying to sound concerned. "Bummer."

"What do you think? Am I messing it up, or what?"

I screwed up my face and pretended to scrutinize the report for several moments. "Gee, Hutch, looks right to me." He didn't know a debit from a credit.

"Well, I like have to figure something out. What should I do?" he asked.

To him, this task was obviously tantamount to quantum physics. I raised an eyebrow and held up one hand sideways to my mouth as if in confidence. "Want to know what I think?" I whispered.

"Yeah." he said and leaned closer.

"Don't turn it in. Same shit happens to me sometimes. So when it does, I just don't turn it in. Don't write the check and no one will be the wiser. Accounting has bigger fish to fry."

He looked as if a great weight had been lifted from his shoulders.

"Hey, cool." he said. He offered me his hand and thanks, and then dismissed me.

A month or so later, he had stopped traveling altogether. When I asked him why, he told me in confidence that he couldn't afford it anymore. I asked how he was going to get around it, since it was a good part of his job, and he just shook his shoulders. "I just hope they're not like 'Hey, what about the money you owe us.'" he said.

But I digress.

As difficult as expense reports were for him, marketing programs were even more complex. In a similar fashion, I misled him so as to totally destroy any credibility he might have had within our organization.

Two months later, Management had given him back his overalls and sent him back to fleet maintenance. They asked if I could take over his duties and I moved into his job. I'd finally figured out how to get up the ladder a rung or two.

When Hutch left, he thanked me profusely, I suppose for all I had done for him.

So after this long diatribe, you're wondering what is the lesson here, right?

First you need to get yourself into a position where you are the doer rather than the doee. Even though you might think that I was a totally rotten son of a bitch, I was really only thinking of the good of the organization. Hutch didn't know a marketing program from his elbow. I did, and was a much better candidate to lead the department than he had been. I just wasn't as young or good-looking. Therefore, if anybody catches you at doing anything like what I did, you can justify it as being for the good of the company. They will then assume that your willfully malevolent behavior was an enlightened means of helping your company's bottom line. This always gets their attention, and excuses anything you do. Remember, the better you are at lying, the better you'll do with upper management. They respect this and value it.

But the real message, is that I finally had started my climb to CEO-dom. And although I didn't concentrate on this in earlier chapters, once I started down this path, I kept doing it and just got better at it.

Exercise:

Develop the following techniques for doing shitty things to the people who work for you as well as your superiors. This includes exit interviews when you are forcing someone out of their job. If you haven't evolved to this state, fire someone every once in awhile so you can get practice. This will put you in the right frame of mind for day-to-day business. Try the following:

- Smile sympathetically; practice this in front of a mirror.
- Say things like; "I regret to inform you." or "you are the most loyal employee I've ever had. Unfortunately, I have no choice but to…"
- Blow your nose while covering your face (this helps if you can't keep a straight face.)
- See if you can cry spontaneously
- If spontaneous crying doesn't work, practice appearing choked up. This is sure fire and you needn't actually shed any tears
- Say how bad you feel about not being able to keep the employee another two weeks until their pension is fully vested.
- Say "what will become of me? At least you know what's going to happen to you." This shifts the sympathy to you.
- Learn how to mis-direct a superior
- Confidentially tell your boss that you heard the CEO talking about canning him.

- Mention that a rival had bad-mouthed him at the company picnic.
- Develop as many other means as you can to develop paranoia in your boss so that you can take his job.

Rose's Rule of Business #19: Animals are not born with a sense of decency and neither are people. It is simply an affectation and must be unlearned if you are to be successful.

Decency presumes a basic benevolence towards other people. This presumption does not exist in business. You can, however, accomplish your goals if you understand this myth, capitalize on it and are perceived to be benevolent, hence decent.

XXIII. Corporate Rank/Accountability

What do you do as a manager when something goes terribly wrong with one of your programs and the shit hits the fan?

It was only a matter of time before the Rhino-Jet 2 fiasco (Chapter XVIII) finally came up in a class action suit. When it did, it only took management a few weeks to find the culprit. I had fully well dodged being blamed for the whole thing. So instead, they pinned it on a floor manager in manufacturing. It probably only would have taken top management a day or two, but we had to wait for them to get back from Florida, where they were all developing new "strategies" in a place of "fresh perspective."

By this time in my career, I understood why they had screwed the floor manager. All she had done was supervise the manufacturing according to proscribed engineering drawings and processes and had actually signed off on them. I, personally, never did. Never mind that many people at various levels of the organization documented the defect, only to have it stopped at the top, and ignored as if it didn't exist.

In fact, during a period of almost a year, people were told point blank not to put anything in writing about the existence of a defect. I believe that one or more of the board had served in minor government positions during the Nixon administration and had learned from this experience. Euphemisms such as "manufacturing tolerances," or "lot differences" were used in any official memos or what passed for documentation.

The clear message from the top down was "This problem doesn't exist. You'd better make it go away, and not let it get to this office."

Many experienced doctors I personally knew called repeatedly, to ask what they were doing wrong with this new product. They had never experienced such a rash of poor results, or complaints from patients.

It was also at this time, that the company put a new interactive voice response and voice mail system on line and this new technology solved the problem of dealing with customers

Mega-Cleft Management felt that this solved the problem, in that it really filtered out a lot of crank calls from these complaining doctors. So the board went back to Florida for the rest of the winter and left the rest of us in charge.

For those calls that got through the system, and without going counter to "party line," or actually saying there was a defect, I found myself SLIMING customers by using terms like "batch variances," and recommending that these doctors revert to the earlier model of Nose Jet, with which we'd experienced no problems. I was enjoying my fluency in SLIME and was having fun giving back to doctors what I had typically gotten from them and their receptionists.

This was where I learned the benefit of rising in corporate rank and subsequently seeing my accountability decline.

When products are recalled, as upper management, you can always find someone at a lower level to take the blame. If defective products are not recalled, customers will eventually stop purchasing them. When layoffs come, you can be sure that it will be because the workers didn't work hard enough, certainly not because management chose the wrong path. Doing this in retrospect can work also. If management really has to take the rap for moving in the wrong direction, but make sure you're at least one level above those blamed.

This principle is **Rose's Law of Relative Accountability** and is demonstrated in the table below.

Rose's Law of Relative Accountability

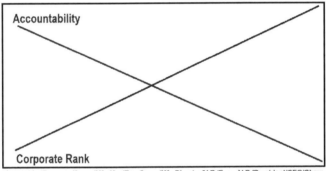

Remember, if you are an executive (V.P. or higher,) you are automatically exempt from any accountability. If you are not a V.P. you need to get really creative about screwing over other people. **How To Blame Others for Your Misdeeds and Make It Stick**, by Orenthal James, is a masterful primer for top business executives. Therefore, be sure that when you start any project you do the following:

- Form a team of at least six people.
- Make sure it's "balanced" for political correctness.
- If you're a woman, make sure you have at least one token male who can take the blame.
- Make sure at least one other member holds a position equivalent to yours in the organization.
- Be sure that there are at least another dozen or so at various steps on the corporate ladder below you.
- Assign responsibilities for all specific tasks to subordinates, then copy the entire team and top management.
- Send lots of progress memos and liberally express concerns. Blind copy your CEO.
- If things start going awry, begin sending the memos jointly with your equivalent.
- When someone comes up with a good idea, express your doubts also.
- Send a memo to the team and blind copy your CEO about the good idea expressing your doubts in the memo, but say that because of the mandate of the team, you will proceed forward. In other words, **Draw a line in the sand and straddle it.**
- If the project succeeds, you're off the hook and can claim credit. If the project fails, you'll be promoted for having foresight and will have already delegated the blame downward with your paper trail.

Exercise:
Having gotten through the earlier principles, this is, perhaps, the easiest exercise of all. In the following space, state three benefits accruing to someone within your company for taking responsibility when something bad happens. (regardless of blame.) [Write Here____]

Rose's Rule of Business #20: It is never the CEO's fault when disaster occurs. It's always the drones who didn't follow instructions or understand their jobs.
Accountability, like responsibility is always delegated downhill when programs fail, regardless of the reason. So make sure you're in a position to do the downward delegating.

XXIV Current Marketing Trends and Other Observations:
Bullshit

Bullshit

Bullshit

Bullshit

Bullshit

Final Exam Exercise:
This one's an open book test.
Determine ten things you can do to become a CEO that you have learned from this book. There are no right or wrong answers.

- If you come up with ten, you win.
- If you come up with less than ten but more than one, you still win, but go back.

Rose's Rule of Business #21: Don't ever write your own Bullshit. Hire the best lawyers to do it for you. They will always find better justifications for whatever you do.

Corporations in America are always looking for some authority to validate the rules by which they operate. Most of it is total Bullshit. Therefore, once you've learned the basics, make your own Bullshit (rules.)

Epilogue
by
Gary L. Rose

From a different perspective, here's what actually happened to the World Famous (at least in Wijgmunt, Indiana) J. Winsted White. After a series of his groundbreaking executive decisions, it culminated in May of 2010. It's all true except for the facts.

J. Winsted White had come from a family of CEO's. The Whites had been numbered among CEO's of some of the most prestigious companies since before the title had come into widespread use in the eighties.

Following in the footsteps of his family predecessors and peers, he had gotten his chance after a long seven year climb to the top of the Hovno Manufacturing Corporation, a wholly owned subsidiary of a Czech conglomerate. He'd clinched the job during a face-to-face interview with all seven of the Schmendricks ("directors" in the Czech language) at a board meeting.

He'd carefully prepared, and knew that he had to win their attention in the first seven-tenths of a second, and not let the interview last for more than five minutes, or he was lost. His life's work would be measured by sound bites.

"So what can you do for us?" the chairman of the Board of Schmendricks asked.

J. Winsted didn't have a clue, but he'd recently been to a creative dissembling seminar and had also remembered what a colleague had told him to say many years ago.

"We've got to bottom-line it, gentlemen." J. Winsted said with great force. "The keys are Minimum investment, Sales Growth, and ROI Next Quarter." he concluded and was silent.

The chairman thought for a moment and then asked "How about ROI the quarter after that?"

"I feel strongly both ways. It's whatever you want." J. Winsted answered.

The Schmendricks quickly looked at each other, and nodded unanimously. "You've got the job." the Chairman of the Board of Schmendricks said.

When he took the helm, the company was doing $200 million in annual sales, and making an annual profit of around twenty-six million dollars. It employed slightly more than two-thousand people.

His first year as CEO, J. Winsted knew that if he fired a bunch of people and cracked the whip really hard, he could show some short-term profits. But he didn't want to use the term "fired" nor did he want to use the phrase "short-term," even though he knew he'd have to pay for the gains somewhere down the line.

So J. Winsted White "outsourced" approximately ten-percent of the work force and contracted with Mini-Fab Co. to farm-out the manufacture of approximately eight-percent of Hovno's total product. He called this "market-sizing," and "synergistic outsourcing." Since Mini-Fab was happy to get the work, they took less profit than they would have normally, in order to get started with Hovno Manufacturing Corporation.

The market-sizing immediately generated $5.5 million. The cost of the outsourced goods came to only $2.7 million, leaving $2.8 million for bottom line profits. Since this represented minimum investment and maximum ROI, it pleased the Board of Schmendricks and they voted J. Winsted a bonus of one million Korunas payable in another twelve months.

The following year, while sales were only up to around $210 million, J. Winsted, went back to the well and outsourced more of his manufacturing. But this time, he got smarter and figured "What the heck, if I can save a bundle by trashing a bunch of lousy workers, what if I trash some of our lousy marketing and sales managers and some of our lousy engineers. After all, they make three, four times what the slobs do."

So he did, and called it "strategic managerial alignment." By now, outsourcing his manufacturing was getting a tad more expensive. Mini-Fab was now producing almost a fourth of J. Winsted's goods, but not as cheaply as before. Nevertheless, J. Winsted was equal to the task. So instead of investing ten million dollars that had been ear-marked for capital goods to keep the manufacturing plant current, he declared a dividend for the stockholders. He also "right-sized" more of the lousy workers. But then he had another inspiration. If he had fewer workers, fewer marketing and sales managers and fewer engineers, he didn't need as many general management or creative people "in-house" either. They could be "out-housed" instead. So now, right-sizing of more workers, plus lousy general management and lousy creative people, dropped another $7 million to the bottom line.

The Board of Schmendricks was tickled and voted J. Winsted twice his previous bonus, this time payable in ninety days, should he choose to do so.

And so it went for several years. Eventually, Hovno Corporation's sales peaked at about two-and-a-quarter billion, while J. Winsted had farmed everything out.

In order to continue dropping money to the bottom line, he had sold most of the company's assets including real estate. After all, since he was no longer manufacturing, he didn't need a plant. He didn't need machinery, so he sold that too.

By renting space in a distribution center, he no longer needed warehouses and sold Hovno's four warehouse buildings.

Since his sales and marketing people were independent contractors, he didn't need vehicles and sold Hovno's fleet, which raised more cash.

His office staff were now all contract employees in virtual offices. This yielded two benefits: He no longer needed to pay benefits, nor did he need a headquarters building. He sold it and rented office space in a furnished office condominium.

He had finally "out-housed" all of his top management, forcing them to pay their own social security, benefits and so forth, so that he wouldn't have to. He had them on hourly contracts, so that he was never more than, let's say, a couple of hours away at the most, from pulling the plug on any of them.

If he could only now figure out how to get Midi-Fab (they had recently changed their name) to do his distribution, he could also get rid of that function.

His organization now looked like this:

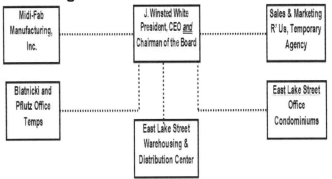

It didn't really bother him that he no longer had any direct reports. It was okay that he had everybody on a dotted line. This maximized his "just-in-time-manufacturing, just-in-time-cash, and just-in-time-firing" functions. He was ready for anything now, and he was proud of himself. He'd watched the stock analysts continue to upgrade Hovno stock and watched its value rise.

But just about the time he had maximized everything, several disturbing occurrences happened simultaneously.

- The non-compete agreement he'd had with Mega-Fab (they'd had another recent name change) ran out. But they had been studying the market and had decided that they were going to make the next generation of products and market them as their own branded products.
- Since J. Winsted had cleverly placed his contracted sales force on a part-time basis, most of them had replaced their income with other sources and were only repping part-time for Hovno.
- The result of the above factors was that when the sales force learned of Mega-Fab's bold intentions, they experienced a crisis of loyalty to Hovno. and bolted (mostly to Mega-Fab's new sales organization.)
- This effectively left J. Winsted without a product to sell, without a sales force to sell it, and without a place to manufacturer it.

- Overnight, the stock price came crashing down.
- All that was left was to turn in the office keys to his landlord.
- J. Winsted was out of a job.

"But aaah... " you think, "J. Winsted still had millions."

Well, not really. J. Winsted had invested his Korunas in Hovno stock and watched its inflated value rise based upon the annual dividends it had paid. Since his greed knew no limits, he had started believing his own press in that he thought the stock would continue to rise. In fact, he had destroyed the organization that had created its real wealth while he had sold off the assets. It was all a house of cards.

The truth was that while J. Winsted thought he was just about the greatest CEO in CEO-dom, he had no engine pulling his stalled train.

To make matters worse, it was only at this point that J. Winsted realized that a Koruna was only a nickel in American money and that what he thought was $3 million, actually only turned out to be about $150,000 US. And this, he had invested in Hovno stock, which was now worthless.

So when the stock came crashing down, as it inevitably had to, J. Winsted was forced to file for unemployment.

"Wait for me Heaves." he said to his chauffeur as he exited the limo at the Unemployment Office.

"Can't, sir. I gotta get this bad boy back to the leasing company or the repo man'll get it and me along with it, and I don't want to walk home. They've been tailing me since yesterday, but I've been able to give 'em the slip. By the way, you'll owe me for another hour." the chauffeur replied. (J. Winsted had him on an hourly also.)

Smartly, J. Winsted took his last roll of bills from his pocket and peeled off six crisp one-dollar bills. "Keep the change." he said and exited.

Once inside, J. Winsted grimaced thinking of the indignity he would suffer just waiting to get this whole employment thing straightened out. Once he got in to see one of the employment agents however, he figured "what the heck, how many CEO's can they have coming in here anyway. I should have this knocked. All I need is one company to be CEO of."

Finally, after a humiliating seven-minute wait, J. Winsted was invited into one of the interviewers' cubes.

"I see you've recently become unemployed, Jonah?" the short, grey-haired chubby man of about sixty asked reading the application in a friendly manner.

"It's J. Winsted White," J. Winsted said, " and I'd prefer it if you called me Mr. White or Sir."

"Certainly, Mr. White or Sir." the employment counselor said respectfully and smiled an understanding smile. "Now I'd like to start by getting a good assessment of your skills so that I can help you find a new job. That is, after all, the first step. Can you give me an idea of what you do?."

"Well, I'm a CEO."

The interviewer, looked at him blankly. After a pregnant pause, he said "Well, yes, of course you are Mr. White or Sir." seeming to humor him. "But can you be a little more specific?"

"Well, I'm not just a CEO, you know. I'm also President, and Chairman of the Board."

The man stared back and made a notation. "Oh... I see. Well, that's very nice, I'm sure, Jon... ah, Mr. White or Sir, but I'm afraid that we'll have to start with something a little more basic. Do you have any marketing skills? Have you ever been in sales? Can you write ad copy?"

J. Winsted just shook his head.

"Can you just tell me if you can do any of the following, and I'll check them off? Can you type, operate a MAC or a PC?"

Again J. Winsted shook his head.

"Do you possess a driver's license?"

Once more J. Winsted shook his head.

"Can you operate any heavy equipment? Do you possess a chauffeur's license? "...perhaps a fishing license...poetic license even..." the seemingly endless list continued.

J. Winsted just shook his head again and finally said, "I have people who do all those things for me." It hadn't sunk in yet that the statement should have been couched in the past tense.

But it finally dawned on him that he was approaching this from the wrong angle. After all, he had lied to his employees, suppliers and stockholders, to get what he wanted, most of all, he had lied to himself. So he had an idea. Falling back on his experience, he realized that lying was the key to everything.

"I'm sorry." he said to the employment counselor. "My mind was elsewhere, and I meant to answer yes. Could you start your list again?"

"Can you operate heavy equipment?"
"Yes."
"Can you operate a PC?"
"Yes."
"Can you do brain surgery?"
"Of course."
"Can you…"

***

Somewhere in an empty house of corporate worship, a voice rang out in darkness in the second decade of the twenty-first century, now referred to as the Dark Ages of Human Commerce.

"All shall be mandated." And thus spake the great corporate god Ci-Eyoh.

And there was silence.

"And all shall be for profits before mine eyes." And thus spake the great corporate god Ci-Eyoh.

And there was silence.

"Where the Hell is everybody?" the great voice rang out.

And there was silence.

And so, the great and good Ci-Eyoh turned on the lights to look into the eyes of his worshipers.

All that remained before him was row upon row of empty cubicles. In the center of each was a spot of ash.

And this angered the good and great Ci-Eyoh. "What...Why...Why have all you disloyal sons of bitches deserted me?" he shouted, creating a great disturbance.

"Because you're a lying sack of shit, you arrogant asshole." said the still, small voice quietly from a corner of the hall. Somehow, it had survived.

A great wind passed accompanied by a loud roar that shook the assembly hall. When it became quiet again, nothing remained at the spot where the good and great Ci-Eyoh stood except a large brown lump and a fetid smell.

"Son-of-a-bitch..." Whispered the still small voice. "...it's about f...ing time."

***

About the Author

Gary Rose spent his first 6 years after University in the United States Air Force. Following, he spent the next 40 working in Corporate America, many of these as a subject matter expert in Corporate Assassinations. Since his (forced) retirement from Corporate America, he considers his association with the once prominent J. Winsted White, if not a true friendship, at least a pleasant acquaintanceship. He also highly prizes being able to host the now indigent White at breakfasts the two men share at a local McDonald's. The two muse over the disparity of their careers and the similarity of their current circumstances.

\#